French Impressions

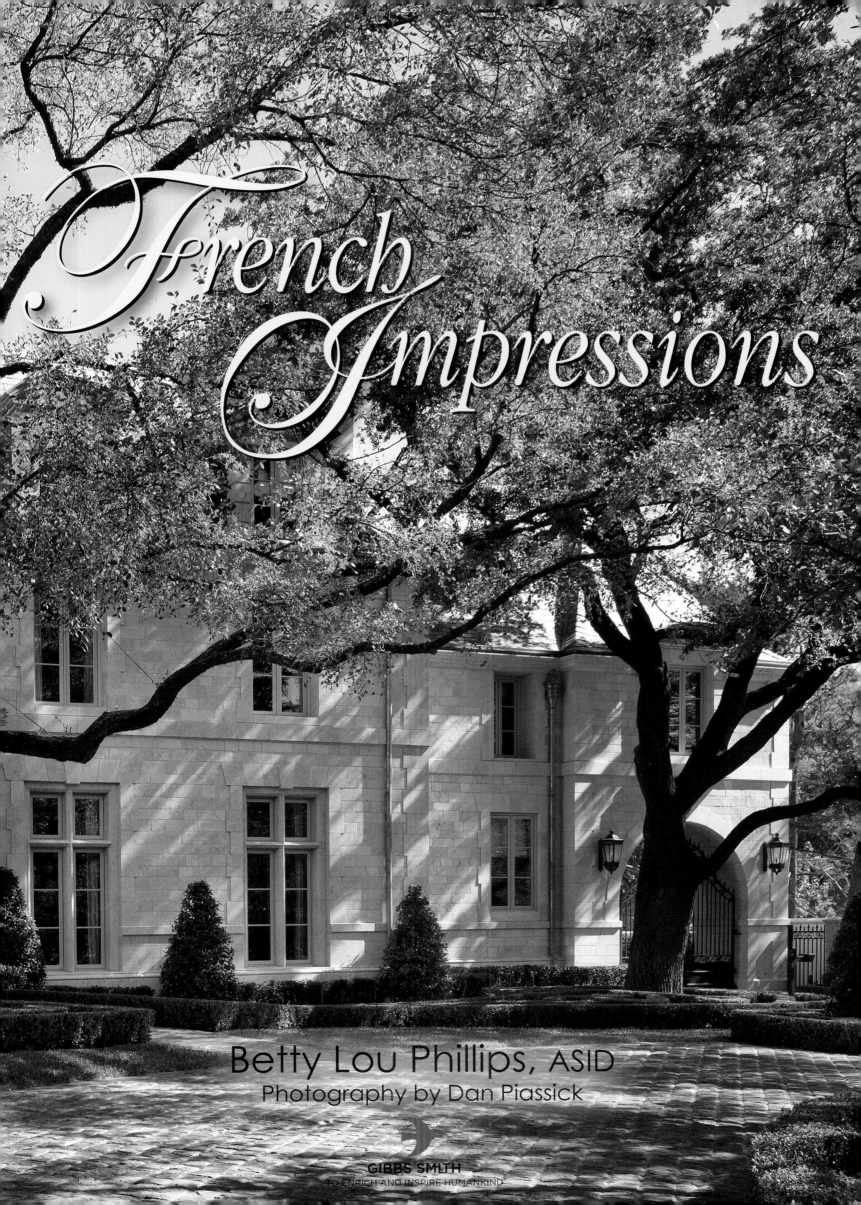

French Impressions

Betty Lou Phillips, ASID
Photography by Dan Piassick

GIBBS SMITH
TO ENRICH AND INSPIRE HUMANKIND

In celebration of American independence, the French erected, in 2006, a ten-foot tall bronze statue of Thomas Jefferson, who served as minister to France from 1784 to1789. The monument stands near the *passerelle de Solférino*, a footbridge in Paris's 7th *arrondissement,* over the River Seine linking the Musée d'Orsay and Jardin des Tuileries. The French credit the third president of the United States with framing them as paragons of good taste when he shipped eighty-six crates of Parisian treasures, including several pieces of famed Sèvres porcelain once owned by Louis XVI, to Monticello, his Charlottesville, Virginia, estate.

"So much of me is made of what I learned from you. You'll be with me like a handprint on my heart."

—from the Broadway musical *Wicked*

CONTENTS

Evoking the élan of France is a soaring, solid oak door that owes its existence to *ébéniste* Bruno Bertoli, who descends from a long line of Italian artisans. *Ébéniste* and its associated forms stem from the word *ébène*, meaning "ebony," since before the abolition of the Parisian guild to which furniture makers belonged (*Corporation des Menuisiers*) only the finest cabinetmakers were entrusted to work with prized, imported ebony. The doorknocker and rim lock are from P. E. Guerin, NYC. Bruno Bertoli can be found near Avignon in the village of Tavel, known for its rosé wines. Authentic Joinery & Millwork in Atlanta represents him in the United States.

ACKNOWLEDGMENTS

Without further delay, I must thank three Bourbon monarchs all named Louis—Louis XIV, Louis XV and Louis XVI—whose passion for beauty helped make the French so French. Merci, merci, merci to them, to the women they married and to a few of their many mistresses.

The ultra luxe Hôtel de Crillon in Paris—where Louis XVI and Benjamin Franklin signed a treaty recognizing the independence of the United States on February 6, 1778—inspired lanterns designed by Larry E. Boerder Architects and fabricated by Iron Age Studios, both of Dallas. Gas lights became a primary source of light after Louis Napoléon Bonaparte III (1852–70), nephew of Napoléon Bonaparte I, hired Georges-Eugène Haussmann (1809–91) in 1853 to oversee the redevelopment and restoration of the French capital, stone by stone.

Also, I am more than grateful to Joan Eleazer and Charles Freeman. Without their assistance and perseverance, this book would not have been possible. But, then, the same can be said for Larry E. Boerder, Ken Harbert, Jeremy Tilley and Adrian Callais, as well as John Sebastian, Tony Weigand, Jim Thompson, Greg Lewis, Colbert Henning, Matt Cain, Jerry Nogalski, Danny Salazar, Harold Leidner, David Newsom and Lance Dickinson.

Also meriting a warm thank-you: Paul Labadie, Tim Morgan, Roy Goldman, Steve Raeborne, Rocky McMinn and John Adams. Taking time from their busy lives, the above went beyond the expected, as did Julie Willenbrock, Christy Gatchell, Esther Gandal, Jim Brown, Jerry Wade, Mark King and Don Schieferecke.

I appreciate the efforts of the following artisans: Deborah Nesbit, Rachel Lea and David Brown, Harold Clayton, Paul Labute, Charlie Peters, Terri Jenny, Greg Bailey, Ruben Sanchez, Gillian Bradshaw Smith, Juan Gonzalas, Allan Rodewald, Jennifer Chapman, Linda Swain, Randy Wenz, Raegan McKinney and Penny Sanders.

Also deserving of thanks: Murielle Abeger, Bruno de la Crois-Vaubois, Patrick McNally, Annick McNally and Thierry Granger.

Without question, I want to thank friend extraordinaire Letitia Jett-Guichard and her reason-for-living-in-France, Alexandre Guichard.

I thank Janice Pedersen Stuerzl for her invaluable research support. Time and again, I thank Andrea Smith for her prized design assistance. And she joins me in thanking our design-savvy team: Brenda Lyle, Kelly Phillips, Katie Howell, Loren Phillips and Molly McGuire. Together we pay homage to Donna Burley, Jesus Marroquin, Daniel Heath, Alan Knight, David Combs, David Peterman, William Kolb, Jewel Bennett, Doreen Wallace, Ana Bohilla, Thomas Johnson, Jeannette Johnson, Diane Lowry, Joe Demoruelle, Jayne Taylor, Nancy Caperton, Stan Brantley, Ellen Nelson, Lisa Frederick, Robert Turner, Britni Brock, Corinthia Runge and Joan Cecil.

Giving credit where due: Lanterns (one unseen) flanking the entrance of the Hôtel de Crillon. Queen Marie Antoinette took piano lessons at the iconic hotel in a room overlooking the Place Louis XV—before it became the Place de la Révolution with the guillotine as its attraction, and then later the Place de la Concorde.

As always, we would like to extend a special thank-you to photographer Dan Piassick. He and his assistants Rusty Bradford and Tiffany Todd helped make our photo shoots successful, interesting—and fun.

Add to the above list appreciation for book designer Cherie Hanson and love for my long-time editor, Madge Baird, and her admirable team. Finally, I sincerely thank you, the reader, for so kindly welcoming French Impressions and my previous design books into your home. Please enjoy.

Layered in French history, a gallery offers a visual feast. Reigning over the eighteenth-century settee, swathed in fabric from Sheila Coombs, is *Marche de Fleurs, Paris*, an oil by French artist Jules-Rene Herve (1871–1981). Handsome *torchieres* (three unseen), a century younger, are from Goodchild Restorations, Dallas. Since the Middle Ages, marmorino plaster—a wall finishing technique that mixes lime and marble dust—has been exuding quiet richness.

INTRODUCTION

For centuries, as we well know, *fine* French furniture in all its forms has been revered by the people of France and adulated by a broad swath of Americans. And little wonder it has held the design world in its thrall. Without question, it is amazingly graceful, actually markedly distinct with carved ornamentation springing from France's twenty-six well-defined regions, where local artisans once passionately reinterpreted the noble style of royal cabinetmakers using local woods and hardware.

A teapot steeped in European allure poses on an antique marble-topped table, evoking the golden age of travel—1900 to 1940. Early in the twentieth century, sturdily plated serving pieces and flatware known by the umbrella term Hôtel Silver were produced for restaurants, railways, ocean liners and grand hotels. Hand-painted *pots de crème*—or cream pots—are from the Hungarian house of Herend. A gift from a friend grew into a collection of the small-lidded pots often used for serving custard, a traditional French dessert.

Predictably, some early furniture was hardly worth writing about. But many other pieces were attention-getting, true works of art, radiating the aristocratic appeal of the French courts while toning down the ostentation that would eventually bring the monarchy to a tumultuous end—in a bloody revolution that began on July 14, 1789, with the storming of the Bastille, a detested Parisian prison.

Yet, pledging *sole* allegiance to fine French furniture—whether crafted during the reign of the *ancien régime* or an era later—has lost some of its luster on our shores. And it's not, like-minded style setters are quick to say, because economic

Across from the formal powder room are four paintings, all the works of H. Claude Pissarro, Camille Pissarro's favorite grandson. A drawing, *Marche au Legumes au Pontoise*, or *Vegetable Market at Pontoise*, by the latter (unseen) adorns the opposite wall. An exceedingly rare set of four eighteenth-century gilt wood Genovese lanterns (three unseen) with Louis XVI–period charm hang in the gallery and hall shown here.

uncertainty is giving luxury a bad name. Despite an ongoing obsession for eighteenth-century rock crystal chandeliers, densely woven tapestries, statuary fit for kings and, for that matter, seeing ourselves in gleaming gilded mirrors, we have developed new appreciation for furnishings from myriad cultures outside the Fifth Republic.

Driven by curiosity in civilizations worldwide, and admittedly, increasingly confident in our own sense of style, no longer are we content with simply raiding France's riches or even splurging on Italy's treasures. With all due respect to both, we trust our instincts to fashion our own global empires of sorts, assimilating influences from the latest stops on our own Grand Tours. But even if traversing continental Europe with our own tutor, chef and valet is out of the question, we now broaden our focus, ultimately displaying open affection for a sea of elements, impressive by any standard, though not necessarily expensive. Never mind that basic French is a requisite for chic urban living. A mix of styles from a mélange of cultures reflects our tastes and sensibilities, at best chronicling our interests and happy experiences.

Statuary from Pittet Architecturals, Dallas, is readily visible from the gallery.

Mirroring the historical differences in Europe and the United States, the eighteenth century meets the twenty-first century and eras in between. Economic crisis or not, we push old-world tradition to new extremes, revealing our innate longings to glam up our impressively French settings with other than the ordinary. For living on this side of the Atlantic means having the freedom to express our individual taste and confidently put our own artistic spin on French style—thereby offering a distinctly different but equally pleasing vision of, dare I say, living royally.

—Betty Lou Phillips, ASID

PS. Yes, at times we clearly bow to the wisdom of Oscar Wilde (1854–1900), who said, "The only way to get rid of temptation is to yield to it." And we find that living royally is not only within our reach but also futile to resist.

Portraits by Carlsbad, California, artist Jennifer Chapman of Louis XV and Madame de Pompadour grace a Cameron Collection loveseat wearing fabric by J. Robert Scott. Born Jeanne-Antoinette Poisson into a family of modest means, the king's influential *maîtresse déclarée*, or officially declared mistress, rose to become a discerning patron of the arts. Not only was she a devotee of the theater and interested in the running of Gobelins, the tapestry workshop, but she also was a passionate promoter of Sèvres porcelain. Despite her detractors, she grew to be a cultural force, prompting a style soon known as *rococo* to spread rapidly throughout eighteenth-century Europe—the most elegant era France has ever known.

Facing portraits of their predecessors are Louis XVI and his fashionable but much-maligned wife, Marie Antoinette, who became queen of France in May 1774 when her nineteen-year-old husband ascended the throne, succeeding his grandfather Louis XV. The Austrian roots of Vienna-born Maria Antonia—the second youngest of sixteen children of Empress Maria Theresa and Emperor Francis I—stirred strong resentment, regardless that her name was changed to Marie Antoinette, the French version of the name, when she arrived in France. Equally troublesome was her blatant resistance to the rigid rules of deportment the court deemed appropriate for royalty. Elisabeth-Louise Vigée-Lebrun was the Queen's favorite portraitist. Portraits by Jennifer Chapman.

VIVE LA FRANCE!

Behold the artistry of the French! In this capricious world, they are keepers of an inimitable style and way of life born centuries ago that will not be subdued by modern forces. No matter that three Bourbon rulers all named Louis with numerals in ascending order unabashedly drenched the Château de Versailles in gilded excess, rousing feelings of resentment outside the palace walls and provoking a torturous uprising that toppled the monarchy. Or that *"liberté, égalité, et fraternité!"* became the national mantra at the onset of the French Revolution and has been heralded ever since. Few would dispute the *ancien régime* still rules, for the indelible imprint left on the nation by Louis XIV (1643–1715) and his descendants Louis XV (1715–74) and Louis XVI (1774–93) is still visible these hundreds of years later.

Striking a dramatic note, a foyer—once the intermediate area between the exterior and interior of a building that between acts offered warmth to theatergoers—reinforces its original function while doubling as a concert hall when strains of Beethoven, Mozart or Bach waft from the Steinway's ivory keys. In the grandest of French *maisons* or *châteaux*, coats are hung in a *vestiaire* (cloakroom); there's no throwing them on the bed. A winding staircase—with subtly glowing medallions evoking Paris's Hôtel de Bonneval that dates back to 1780—sweeps up to the second floor, connecting an *enfilade* of noble-sized rooms. Steps above the rest: seventeenth-century stone from Paris Ceramics USA, New York.

LEFT: Steeped in beauty, a tiered, nineteenth-century *lustre candelabrum*—chandelier with crystal pendants—nearly eight feet tall and five feet wide is suspended above a sweeping staircase after journeying from a palatial casino in Deauville, the glamorous seaside resort on France's northern coast long famed for its racecourse. A young Gabrielle "Coco" Chanel (1883–1971) opened a millinery shop in Deauville in 1913, years before giving the world the little black dress and Chanel No. 5 perfume, which to this day is the world's top-selling fragrance. For motorized lifts, look to Aladdin Light Lift, www.aladdinlightlift.com. And for chandeliers with a grand past—restored from faded glory—look to J. P. Carpentier at the Marché Serpette in the famous Marché aux Puces, Paris.

BELOW: Nineteenth-century children's chairs have more than a modicum of style, especially when impeccably dressed in a Cowtan & Tout check and Marvic stripe. Gimp is from Samuel & Sons.

FACING: Rough-cut stone walls edged in smooth quoins, reclaimed stone flooring and regal nineteenth-century *torchères* (torch lights) discovered at Goodchild Restorations, Dallas, deftly emit the air of a majestic *château*. Seventeenth-century first face Blond Barr, varying in tone from cool cream to dove gray to warm honey, was shipped from France to Paris Ceramics USA, NYC. First face, or first cut, salvaged limestone has the aged patina that the other cut layers do not, though they, too, are worthy of admiration.

FRENCH IMPRESSIONS

To be sure, each of the Bourbon monarchs had his own set of admirers and detractors; but it is safe to say, Louis XIV deserves credit for influencing most everything the French do. For, once the Sun King and his court had settled in to the sumptuous seventeenth-century splendor of Versailles—with its more than 700 rooms, 2,153 windows, 67 staircases and 352 *cheminées*—he ordered that the doors of his father's transformed hunting lodge be flung open to those who lived a bit more modestly. And with that, he astounded the world with France's masterful artisanship, setting standards of excellence previously unseen in Italy and Spain. As if leaving nothing to chance, he also offered a guide to the French *art de vivre*, or art of living, which would inspire generations of tastemakers who, in turn, would bring the country further global acclaim.

ABOVE: A longing for uncommon beauty, for the right price, led to the design of the mailbox here after noticing a letterbox with the words *buca per le lettere* gracing a palazzo in Verona, Italy. Iron Age Studios fabricated the *boîte aux lettres*.

FACING: "*Très Chic*," an Ashford Court toile, envelopes a mail room, taking the hassle out of traveling to some of the world's most renowned sites, such as the Eiffel Tower, which celebrated its 121st birthday in 2010. Interestingly, the iconic symbol of Paris was not always beloved. Reportedly, outrage surrounded its selection as the centerpiece of the 1889 Paris Exposition Universelle.

An artfully fashioned staircase rises to the occasion, dressed for the season. Europeans have long coveted noble, hand-woven tapestries, probably ever since 1662, when Louis XIV founded the royal manufactory Gobelin. In the late fifteenth century, the aristocracy used them to insulate damp walls of their *châteaux* and castles. These days, Americans often have them at the top of acquisition lists.

FACING: As the holidays approach, this *maison* takes a minimalist approach, much like the broad, tree-lined Champs-Élysées, which gleams with white lights. In French homes, trees often remain lit until the Feast of the Epiphany, which is the twelfth day after Christmas and the religious observance of the three kings visiting the infant Jesus. Here, Fraser firs glisten thanks to the efforts of designer Raegan McKinney at Todd Events, Dallas.

Quite clearly, Louis XIV's extravagance did not go unnoticed. Nor was the excess that reigned quickly forgotten by taxpayers, who deeply resented supporting his lavish lifestyle and his more than a dozen mistresses. Of course, not all the king's loyal subjects, anymore than his foes, could, or wanted to, emulate *la grandeur* of Versailles. But even those who denounced its size and gasped at the opulence were impressed by the Sun King's perfectionism. Elevating him to a symbol of stylistic authority, they magnified his presence in the world by becoming products of their environment, knowingly or not. From an insistence on finely crafted furniture and regal textiles to turning out rooms with dignity and panache, the people's unparalleled attention to detail—which today borders on obsession—is a testament to the late king's fastidiousness.

These days, the French like to think that a sense of style is in their genes, a gift inherited, passed down from generation to generation. And perhaps this is true—for like father, like son; like mother, like daughter. The trait runs deep, although it may be honed in childhood, when children learn to appreciate the splendor of the commonplace, the elegant and the antique. Behind most every heavy, imposing door lies a certain *je ne sais quoi*, or indescribable attribute, that parents feel a responsibility to pass on, giving their children an edge from the cradle onward, and spurring our sense of wonderment over and over again. >33

A snow-dusted elm limb outlines the front door, as if confirming that architect Larry E. Boerder chose the perfect spot to site the entrance of this *château*.

Fortuny's burnished copper and bronze *Sévigné* swathes tables laden with masses of black pussy willows from Avant Garden, Dallas. Master craftsman Paul Labadie hand-carved the *boiserie*. The walls—hand-finished by Sanders Studio, Dallas—brim with lithographs by Impressionist artist Pierre Auguste Renoir (1841–1919).

Taking his cue from the French, Dallas artisan Paul Labadie painstakingly sculpted delicate low relief ornamentations in quartersawn oak after meticulously planning each section. He then hand-scraped the wood and framed the *boiserie* panels individually, assuring the wood would have space to expand and contract when the temperature and humidity dipped or climbed. Finally, he hung each panel on French cleats, isolating it from the wall—stepping one panel forward and the next back, confident the cleats would keep the panels stable when taking their place around the perimeter of the room. If antique walls could talk, they'd point out that this explains how *boiserie*, popular in seventeenth- and eighteenth-century French interiors, survived moves from one location to another, if not rescued from demolished castles.

FACING: Impressive by day, a dining room becomes glamorous at night when three round tables tempt guests with the warmth of a fire in the coldest months, and year-round with regally hand carved *boiserie*—the French term for floor-to-ceiling carved wood wall paneling. Buccellati sterling silver vessels, filled with clouds of blue hydrangeas by Randy Wenz at Avant Garden, Dallas, top Coraggio Textiles' rich copper tablecloths. Taking the room from romantic to dramatic: a pair of gold and crystal *lustres*—chandeliers—circa 1850, happened upon in Bordeaux, and a like chandelier found in Paris more than a year later.

The carved foliage of a Renaissance *cheminée* that once stood in a Loire Valley *château* inspired the finials on page 34. Candlesticks holding court on the mantel are antique.

Yes, we are struck by the flair of the French, reflecting their self-assured approach to design, glamorous culture and lasting respect for the past. It not only captures our attention but also inspires us to channel our energies in pursuit of their strategy for making a statement. Of course, style is easy to recognize. Clarifying it can be more challenging.

So, what is style? Webster defines it as "a distinctive manner of expression," thus leaving the word open to interpretation.

À la française, unpretentious *parquet de Versailles* worn-wood floors from Galerie Origines, Paris, mirror the past.

In a lot of minds, style is an unerring instinct, as well as a way of life, that prizes quality and flows from a penchant for detail. Others see it as the discreet air of *savoir-faire*—*savoir* meaning "to know" and *faire* "to do"—sophistication and culture, emanating from within and subtly revealing itself in unassuming ways of living, decorating and entertaining. Still others—many others—believe it is a dash of attitude bound with old-world elegance, giving life to the past while bringing understated luxury to rooms.

Say what you like, style is not an easy attribute to come by, which is no doubt the reason we look to the French, who seemingly exude it with ease.

To be sure, neither social standing nor money offers any guarantee of style. It cannot be procured locally, on the Internet or even on the moon; nor can it be had from a recipe or via celebrity status. So the French—standard bearers of style *par excellence*—have become our templates for good taste, luring us with their air of superiority, famous reserve and example. For them, turning heads is second nature, thanks to the lofty way their priorities are reflected not only in what they wear or the confident manner in which they move, but also in the careful way they present themselves to the world. >49

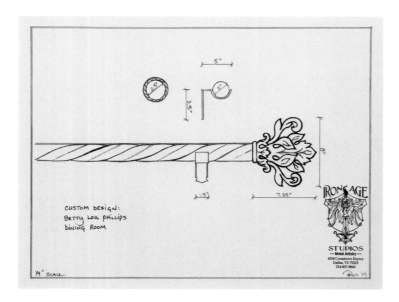

Noble-sized finials were fashioned by Iron Age Studios using an age-old process called *repoussé*—a technique whereby a malleable metal is ornamented and shaped by hammering from the reverse side. *Passementerie*—tassels, braids, fringes and tieback trimmings from the French *passement*, a strip of lace—by Janet Yonaty, West Hollywood, adds to the beauty of Coraggio Textiles' sumptuous silk curtains that float from iron rods (one unseen). Straight Stitch, Dallas, produced the *haute* treatment.

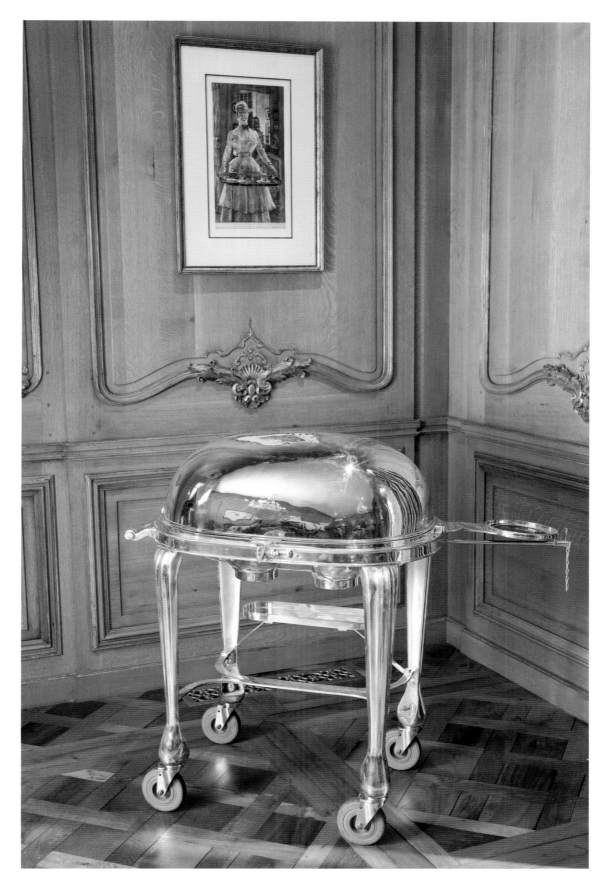

With the elegance of another era, a Hôtel Silver trolley, circa 1935, with fluted legs adds to the room's cachet. At formal French dinners, etiquette dictates that the hosts sit facing each other at the center of the table—rather than at the head of the table—with guests seated in order of importance, starting on the host and hostess's right and left. Those youngest—or those young and unmarried—sit at the ends of the table. Since many French are superstitious, they will often go to extremes to avoid the discomfort of having thirteen at a rectangular table. Inviting six, ten, fourteen or eighteen guests—not eight, twelve or sixteen—also assures that men and women alternate on either side of the hosts. This is to say that a round table is more conducive to conversation than one large rectangular one and point out that power seating is not an issue.

Many consider Herend's "Rothschild Bird" the embodiment of hand-painted porcelain. Created for Europe's Baron de Rothschild family, twelve diverse motifs tell the nineteenth-century tale of the baroness's lost pearl necklace, which was found when the gardener spotted birds in a tree playing with it at the Rothschilds' Vienna residence. Flatware is by the Italian House of Buccellati.

Inspired by characters from Tchaikovsky's *Nutcracker Suite*, Limoges porcelain firm Bernardaud sends a happy holiday message via toy soldiers, wooden horses and Christmas trees on "Grenadiers" dinner service. In France, water and wine goblets meet directly above each plate, rather than above the knife and spoon, as in the States.

OPPOSITE, ABOVE LEFT: Every French dinner, whether a family affair or a *grand dîner*, begins with an *entrée*, or first course—called an appetizer in this country. The thinking is that a simple salad or a small bowl of soup will effectively slow the meal and let the brain catch up with the stomach. At dinner parties one normally serves oneself the main course, which means being in control of the portion. And not surprisingly, heaping a plate with food is extremely bad manners. China is "English Renaissance" by Royal Doulton.

OPPOSITE, ABOVE RIGHT: Fine dining becomes even finer when a table is set with Wallace's "Grand Baroque" flatware, Saint-Louis's "Tommy" crystal, and Bernardaud's "Grand Versailles" china. The latter salutes the seat of power from 1682 until the French Revolution in 1789, borrowing hues from silks, embroideries and trims that embellished rooms of the royal *château*. No matter that opulent entertaining fell from favor when the monarchy came tumbling down. By 1800, it was again fashionable.

Keeping pace with Paris, place cards indicate where each guest is to sit. And centerpieces are low so they do not interfere with conversation. In many Parisian restaurants, the chef is responsible not only for the cuisine but also for the flowers, china, glassware, cutlery and linens.

When a *palazzo* (palace, literally), in a bend of Venice's Grand Canal, exports inspiration, it is only fitting that a palette of platinum and gold garners admiring glances. Adding to this stateside salon's old-world graciousness: soaring 14-foot ceilings, reclaimed patterned oak *parquet de Versailles* floors from Galerie Origines, Paris, and *portes-fenêtres* (French doors) awash in fabric by Manuel Canovas. Nancy Corzine chairs in the style of Louis XVI wear Scalamandré textiles. The *crémone* bolts from P. E. Guerin, NYC, could almost pass for artwork. Bestowing further nobility: an Oushak rug, circa 1890, with worn and faded beauty, happened upon at Moattar, Ltd., Atlanta. Baccarat's *photophore clairs*, or clear votives, are by Philippe Starck for Neiman Marcus. Most all other accessories are less-than-haughty antiques.

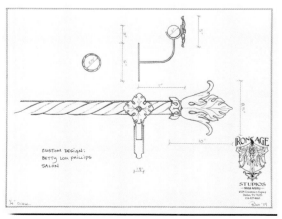

Tossing aside any preconceived ideas of what a finial should look like results in one that takes its cue from the 18th-century limestone *cheminée* (fireplace) that once resided in the salon of a small *château*. The unassuming fireplace was unearthed at DHS Designs in Annapolis, Maryland.

While Marie Antoinette's fondness for neoclassical furnishings, such as these burnished salon chairs, hardly robbed the palace of glamour, it was not until Empress Eugénie (1826–1920), the elegant wife of Napoleon III, revived the style that people would credit Marie Antoinette with building the design's cachet. A walnut armoire, circa 1780, stands well above the fray. Yet looks are not everything. Whether modest or magnificent, the point of pride confirming value and status is *provenance*—a document authenticating origin and chronicling previous ownership, including identifying the experts who have vetted the piece in the past. Even an armoire that might not ordinarily merit a second look commands respect when accompanied by a paper trail of its riveting history.

A former tablecloth brings Italian chic to a French chair and at the same time advertises the resident's weakness for words, to say nothing of poetry.

LEFT: A fittingly feminine, fashionable library holds sprawling collections of art, architecture, textile and design books, some long out of print. Volumes also reflect an interest in French and Italian gardens. Looking as if fabricated by one of France's *petits mains*—the highly skilled tailors who hand-stitch *haute* couture ball gowns—is the billowing, floor-sweeping window treatment embellished in Christopher Hyland trim, intricately constructed by Straight Stitch, Dallas. The nineteenth-century Empire chandelier from Ainsworth-Noah, Atlanta, assuredly casts its own light on European culture, as Luigi Loir's (1845–1916) *Rendezvous in the Park*, an oil on canvas in its original 18-karat gold frame, looks over reclaimed oak flooring from Galerie Origines, Paris. The area rug is a work of art from Matt Cameron Rugs & Tapestries that pays homage to the visions of Mariano Fortuny.

"Your library is your portrait," British bibliophile Holbrook Jackson pithily pointed out in the nineteenth century. And, so, a room that is warm and inviting is as organized as the Library of Congress, speaking volumes. Meanwhile, upholstery impeccably dressed in Fortuny adds a layer of luxury. A Louis XV writing desk from Country French Interiors, Dallas, stands behind the sofa in place of a table. The antique oak floor—dents and all—was imported from France and laid in a chevron pattern.

FRENCH IMPRESSIONS

Not surprisingly, then, their homes are chicly rendered works of art, impressively composed. Exuding a passion for beauty, an intuitive sense of scale, harmony of color and expression of one's inner self, interiors vary widely, taking shape according to one's definition of style while offering a window into the soul. Indeed, there are no so-called rules. Yet, seemingly, all have the same *raison d'être*. Exhibiting a reverence for the past, they highlight the French way of life with its matchless mix of simplicity, elegance and grace.

Grandchildren now enjoy *Make Way for Ducklings*, *Mudlark*, *Ferdinand the Bull* and the *George* and *Martha* books beloved by their parents. Hundreds more favorites stand waiting to be picked up.

FACING: Giving a library with old-world élan new perspective is a file room behind closed doors.

Wrapped in detail, antique furnishings—exquisite tapestries, dramatic chandeliers and storied armoires—share space with the new, and swaths of luxurious fabrics mingle with more textured ones, all from prestigious European mills. There is a subtle blend of the expensive and the less costly, regardless if notably absent is furniture dripping in gold leaf. *Passementerie*-embellished curtains flow from iron rods as understated alternatives to the heavy, over-the-top window treatments that are so twentieth-century. Meanwhile, unexpected hints of glamour fashion an interesting, artful mood.

Attended or not, an elevator can readily whisk overnight guests struggling with laptops and luggage to their appropriate floors. The nineteenth-century Baccarat chandelier was discovered on a buying trip to the City of Light. To curb the importation of glassware from Bohemia and other countries, plus generate new jobs, the Bishop of Metz founded a glass factory in 1765 in the village of Baccarat, some 150 miles east of Paris. Proximity to the forest made the location ideal for powering the furnaces needed when making windowpanes, mirrors, bottles and stemware.

Indeed, interiors are at once comfortable and meaningful yet laced with the feeling of unassuming splendour—the very traits that offer ample proof of not only taste but of the creative power and cultural force Louis XIV to this day triumphantly exerts—as he no doubt intended.

Today the upscale Musée des Cristalleries de Baccarat is centrally located—at 11, place des Etats-Unis 75116 in the French capital—and houses a swank restaurant designed by Philippe Starck. Since all addresses in central Paris start with 75, it is easy to learn which of the twenty *arrondissements*, or districts, a building is in; all one need do is look at the last two digits of the postal code. The Baccarat Crystal Museum, for example, is in the 16th, which would often be abbreviated 16th Arr. or 16eme. The French abbreviate much the same way we do. Here, sixteenth, for example, is shortened by using the number 16 and the last two letters of the word "sixteenth," becoming 16th. French for sixteenth is sèizieme, thus written 16eme. In France, it is common to abbreviate by using the last one, two or three letters in a word.

RIGHT: Fashioned from silk, Janet Yonaty's luxurious tassel incorporates crystals. Drapery rod is from Manor House in Collierville, Tennessee.

FACING: Orchestrated walls, upholstered in bolts of Christopher Hyland linen, serve as canvas for composer Wolfgang Amadeus Mozart (1756–91), who wrote more than 600 works during his lifetime. His most famous operas include *The Marriage of Figaro*, *The Magic Flute* and *Don Giovanni*. Also, he is famous for his *Requiem Mass*. Adding to the elegant tone is a pair of mirrors from Le Louvre Antiques, Dallas, and Sherle Wagner's 24-karat gold-plated fixtures, plus her white onyx pedestal sinks and wastebaskets. High-quality onyx is Karchi, Pakistan's pride. At Versailles, Marie Antoinette's distinct fondness for roses was apparent; they would become one of her personal symbols.

BELOW: A lyrical motif, circa 1780, sets the tone, heralding a love of music. The Patina chest, hand-painted in Italy, is in perfect harmony. Historical antique instruments wait for a new home in Paris at Orphée (8th Arr.).

A TASTE FOR PARIS

France abounds with a mix of restaurants, brasseries, cafés and bistros, some more haughty than humble, many capable of luring gourmands the world over, even sans Michelin stars. But in the gastronomically obsessed French capital—where there is more than a hint of snobbery—one does not "eat," one "dines." Certainly, one can "eat" an apple, a piece of perfectly ripened domestic cheese or a perfectly browned baguette fresh from the *boulangerie* (bakery), just never a meal. It is always, "Where did you dine?" not, "Where did you eat?" >62

Time marches on—across gleaming Calacatta Vision marble walls, tiled in a staggered pattern, and up sculptured marble moldings. Meanwhile, warm gray cabinetry glazed to perfection by Sanders Studio, Dallas, caters to a sophisticated palette. Parisian clock is from Ronnie & Guy Weil Antiques, New Hope, Pennsylvania. (Historians and European purists maintain that IIII is the proper way to represent 4 o'clock.) Brazil's Beleza soapstone countertop looks up to a collection of Hôtel Silver with some pieces from Le Meurice in Paris, others from Claridge's in London.

No matter that the impeccably crafted La Cornue range appealed to Impressionist artist Claude Monet, whose kitchen at Giverny flaunts the same "Château" range. Its beauty also stirred animators of the Disney movie *Ratatouille*. Taking the latter seriously resulted in a commercial kitchen far above the ordinary. The oversized culinary utensils are from E. Dehillerin in Paris, which has been catering to equipment needs of France's chefs for nearly two centuries. Lighting fixtures are from Ann-Morris Antiques, NYC. Samuel & Sons' crystal beaded ball fringe garnishes Osborne & Little fabric on windows. Wheatgrass lines the marble windowsills.

A vintage sieve that looks as if it came from a kitchen supply store is, however, from Brendan Bass, Dallas, and is prepared to act as a filter, separating solids from liquid.

FACING: In a well-equipped kitchen, a thick slab of soapstone tops a large central island. Why soapstone? It is nonporous, so extremely dense that it does not harbor bacteria. Also, it is heat resistant and family friendly and requires low maintenance. The dramatic floor is Thar Stone—black limestone from Rajasthan, India, mined deep in the Thar Desert bordering Pakistan. Satisfying even the most discerning gourmand is fabric from Pierre Frey, covering bar stools by Michael Shannon & Associates, San Francisco. Fluted plates and bowls are from Bergdorf Goodman, NYC. Sub-Zero's glass-front refrigerator makes it easy to scan contents without wasting energy.

In high style, rattan baskets hold an assortment of cloth napkins and napkin rings.

FACING: At the center of it, is Hôtel Silver—a tray and disparate elements—garnished with Royal Doulton's Hotel china. Sumptuous sweets accompanied by over-the-top artistry are from Dallas Affaires Cake Company (www.Dallasaffairescakeco.com). Bar stools wear John Hutton slipcovers.

Those with innate Gallic style do not attempt to mask *l'esprit parisien*—that is, an air of superiority attributable to living in the hub of much of France's cultural, educational, financial and political power. As it is, nowhere in the republic drives public taste more passionately than the capital, the most populous and the wealthiest area of France. In Paris, communicating with heightened sophistication speaks of high birth, which is the hope.

This is not to say that reveling in the status that living in Paris brings, any more than mirroring the behavior of the aristocracy, necessarily supports claims of noble ancestry. Having the "nobiliary" particle "de" in one's last name can tip the odds in one's favor yet still does not guarantee royal lineage. But then, this is almost beside the point, since exuding pomposity reminiscent of those at court— the most refined and cultured in all of Europe—alone boosts one's standing on France's complex social scale. Suffice it to say, officially, the Revolution swept away the aristocracy. However, few people are as caste-conscious as the French.

(In the interest of equality, the Fifth Republic ideal ignores religious and ethnic differences so those with residency papers exude a collective identity regardless of their origins. Officially, all 65 million citizens are French, neatly grouped, whether they share or distance themselves from Gallic values and obligations.)

With a collection of antique copper pots and pans in the kitchen, there is no excuse for ordering in or even picking up takeout. Warm, glazed finish on cabinets creates the illusion of age. Pressed tin ceiling is from W. F. Norman Corp., Nevada, Missouri.

In France, professional chefs call it *mise en place*—everything in its place. Within easy reach are culinary tools with Brazilian rosewood handles and solid brass rivets by La Cornue.

Yet blatantly stating that one descends from a titled family is not looked upon favorably, any more than brazenly parading one's wealth like the Bourbon monarchs or their wives and many mistresses. And though in all French dictionaries the terms *noble* and *aristocrate* are now synonymous, titles often carry little weight given that Napoléon conferred them overly freely after crowning himself emperor. Truth is, Parisians regularly wonder who was born a noble and who was handed a title.

Regardless, anybody who is anybody is aware that there *are* socially acceptable ways of letting others know that one indeed has a drop of noble blood—short of having the country's social registry, *Le Bottin Mondain,* hand-delivered to their door. Thinly veiled allusions to the family *château,* the property in Corsica, the *mas* in Provence or the chalet in Gstaad imply that one has a history, which is a start. It is also fine to mention how much time one spends there, but never, ever what it is worth unless intending to sell it.

A catering kitchen gleams with the help of Calacatta Vision slab countertops quarried in Italy, a slim Sub-Zero and stainless steel cabinets, some with glass. Three factors determine the quality of stainless: the thickness of the steel, the nickel content and the finishing technique. Recommended for residential use are 18, 20 or 22 gauge steel—and a brushed finish, as it is easier to care for than a polished sheen. An Osborne & Little sheer adorns the window with Samuel & Sons glass trim, doubled. Crémone bolt is from P. E. Guerin, NYC.

Tellingly, too, eighteenth-century furniture, posh textiles, distinctive porcelains and oil paintings in original carved-wood frames are instantly identifiable indicators of style and station. Much like the fine linens and heirloom silver passed down from one generation to the next, all are celebrated badges of the fortunate, having bearing on how one is perceived.

Its Christmas-tree shape and fresh fragrance make the rosemary tree an ideal holiday decoration.

In matters material, however, nothing manages to vault those with the patina of privilege to the top of the social pyramid quite like dwelling in an elegant Haussmann-era *hôtel particulier* converted to *appartements* with fourteen-foot ceilings, deep chiseled moldings, patterned wood floors and imposing fireplaces—even if missing many other accoutrements stateside luxury residences demand. Of course, not everyone can live within blocks of the Louvre, let alone in such imposing architectural grandeur. But frankly, evidence suggests that many Parisians are less interested in elevating their status by perching in the epitome of old-world elegance than intent on being recognized and admired for their royal roots.

FACING: Adding spice are Viking's 36-inch sleek, freestanding gas range and Kitchen Aid's candy red mixer.

ABOVE: Parisian or not, many find *escargots de Bourgogne*—snails topped with parsley and garlic butter, and cooked in their shells—difficult to resist.

LEFT: Linen napkins—lace trimmed and elaborately embroidered—first appeared in Rheims, France, reportedly in the court of Charles VII (1429–61). By the seventeenth century, servants were folding *serviettes* into exquisite shapes depicting boats, swans, birds, flowers and more. When it came to folds, ways varied, but the protocol for napkin use was single fold—as the exalted French court of Louis XV imposed strict rules of conduct on the aristocracy. "It is ungentlemanly to use a napkin for wiping the face or scraping the teeth, and a most vulgar error to wipe one's nose with it," a 1729 treatise proclaimed. And whether a tad obsessive or not, "The person of highest rank in the company should unfold his napkin first, all others waiting till he has done so before they unfold theirs. When all of those present are social equals, all unfold together, with no ceremony."

Fortunately, there is no shortage of class markers, fitting conveniently within approved boundaries without breaking unwritten French codes. And given the country's reputation for fine cuisine, to say nothing of lives more gracious and less hurried than our own, it comes as no surprise that polished table manners often are an indication of patrician lineage, though it would be . . . well, tasteless for a Parisian to say so.

Most know that brewing the perfect cup of espresso is a talent that starts with a machine scrupulously clean and a cup with thick walls and narrow mouth to retain the heat and aroma.

It is entirely apt, then, that the word *étiquettes* is French, translating as ticket, label and tag. According to a tale that leaves some questions unanswered, Louis XIV's royal gardener erected signs in the exquisite formal gardens of Versailles aimed at keeping the aristocrats from trespassing. When ignored, the Sun King decreed that no individual was to drift beyond the bounds of *étiquettes*. Later, the declaration came to include established rules of court conduct, or protocol synonymous with etiquette that seemingly has not waned.

The only way to get rid of temptation is to yield to it"

Oscar Wilde (1854-1900)

Quality appliances, cookware and knives, along with dinnerware, glasses, flatware, cookbooks and table linens, are all fundamental to a kitchen. But one can hardly stop there, not when it is important that the pantry have a charm equal to other parts of the home.

SAUCE TOMATE / KETCHUP

CAFÉ / COFFEE

PAIN / BREAD

CRAQUELINS / CRACKERS

CHIPS / POTATO CHIPS

EPICES / SPICES

CÉRÉALES / CEREALS

In a city filled with legendary shopping, it is impossible to say where in Paris one came across the magnetic French board. It is, however, worth remembering that the Marché Biologique, or Organic Market, on the Boulevard Raspail, is one of the best of Paris's outdoor markets.

However modern this age, daily life reflects more than a *soupçon* of tradition. Befitting the courts of the *ancien régime,* an ardently embraced formality lingers. No tasteful dinner party is complete without breathtaking silver, glistening crystal, oversized white linen napkins, and a regal mix of memorable china integral to the table's beauty.

Nevertheless, a Parisian will say, "It will just be a simple dinner," when extending an invitation to a candlelight fête designed to please the senses as much as the palate. But, of course, it will not. How could it be in a country that not only produces praiseworthy wines but also an abundance of fresh produce, tempting breads and more than 350 different cheeses from the various regions, to say nothing about astonishingly rich chocolates? Or where hosts pour energy into dressing their tables with a virtuous mix of panache and simplicity, taste and resourcefulness that is at once inviting, surprising and inspiring? But, then, the French are fond of the word *simple*. To them, it is chic beyond words, along with exquisite taste, impeccable manners and decorous sociability. Without question, all exude an elitist persona—an end in itself.

Though classic, a powder room emits a bit of attitude. The subtle sheen of dove gray wall covering from Pollack complements Waterworks' sparkling white Thassos, a water jet–cut marble from Greece that looks as if chiseled. Flat pieces are polished. French chandelier from Marvin Alexander, NYC, is circa 1900.

The Revolution curbed fancy in-home dining. With most upper-class fortunes lost or clearly dwindled, there was little work in the residences of those with noble lineage. Suddenly *haute* cuisine became available in *"les grands restaurants"* in Paris and nearby cities as more than a few chefs opened relatively elegant dining spots. At a round table perfect for dining *en famille*, vegetable garden markers serve as place cards.

RIGHT: Napkin rings were first used in France around 1800. Between washdays, each family member typically stored his or her own napkin in a *serviette* ring. These days, a grasshopper securing a napkin is guaranteed to bring a smile. In many countries, grasshoppers are symbols of good luck.

FACING: Rich walnut paneling and tall steel Crittal windows imported from England frame an artfully designed breakfast room, which overlooks the gardens. Smocked curtains wear Sanderson gingham, while Nobilis trims Christopher Hyland sheers. Gerbera daisies top a Portuguese dining table by Michael Taylor resting on reclaimed wood floors from Galerie Origines, Paris. The iron chandelier is old.

Table Manners

While *specialties de maison* vary with seasonal loyalty to regionally produced ingredients, the unspoken rules governing dinner parties, for the most part, remain unchanged. Becoming familiar with the manners and mores of the French could be embarrassment saving, or simply alleviate any anxiety. Here are a few basics, some well known, others perhaps not:

⚜ Be aware of the fifteen-minute rule. Forget that Louis XIII said, "*La ponctualité est la politesse des rois,*"—punctuality is the politeness of kings. If asked to arrive at eight, appear *exactly* fifteen minutes after the appointed hour. Do not arrive any earlier or more than five minutes later.

⚜ Know that the era's all-around, no-fail, forever correct hostess gift is a small but strikingly packaged, costly box of chocolates, which will often be opened and shared when coffee is served. Never, ever walk through the door with an armful of cut flowers demanding attention. It is not the moment. Instead, consider sending flowers the morning of the party or as a thank-you the day after the event, keeping in mind that Parisians tend to favor the same blossom *en masse*. But, of course, chic florists in the French capital know that. Alternatively, if hand delivering a bouquet of long-stemmed roses, be aware that it is important to remove the thorns.

Aptly known as the "Prada for Pets," Les Cadors boutiques in the Marais and Saint Germain stock Swarovski-studded collars, faux fur coats and lynx-upholstered sofas, while nearby *la pâtisserie pour chien* offers *foie gras* and carob truffles. Doting parents spare no expense pampering their beloved *chien* with thalasso therapy and aqua massages. A. D. Prince also offers color restoration for faded coats. The lavish spoiling of dogs, called *toutoumania*, is central to the French culture.

❧ In keeping with tradition, greet the hosts by proffering kisses on alternating cheeks, starting with their right cheek. Although it is common to offer four kisses in some parts of France, in and around Paris, doing so is thought *déclassé*.

❧ Once, the kitchen in most *châteaux* was the exclusive domain of the household staff, or the *personnel,* as they were and are called. Though the Revolution was centuries ago, the French still cannot envision people gathering in this space. Therefore, only if the hostess is a very good friend who is not assisted by a chef, is it permissible to ask if it is possible to help in some way. But should one walk into the kitchen to do so? Ummm . . . no.

❧ A *grand dîner,* intended to be savored over several hours, debuts with an *entrée*—the entry into a meal—followed by the *plat principal* or *plat de résistance* (main course), *salade* (salad, greens tossed with vinaigrette to cleanse the palate), *fromage* (cheese) and dessert. Although we think of the *entrée* as the main course, it is the first course in France.

❧ It is considered unforgivably rude not to devote equal time engaging the *invité* on both the left and right in conversation. However, do not ask a person's occupation, or inquire where he lives. As it happens, the French deem both questions highly personal.

At the Université du Vin, on the grounds of the Château Suze-la-Rousse in France's Rhône-Alps region, wine lovers from around the world have been honing their skills while learning about the complexities of French wines since 1978. The school offers graduate and postgraduate courses in the art of being a sommelier, as well as short courses for wine merchants, bartenders and those who are simply interested in wine.

High ceilings, antique wood beams and a sixteenth-century heavily carved, walk-in limestone *cheminée* from R.F. Imports, Dallas, fuses the charm of rural France with the unmistakably urbane sensibilities of Paris. Drenching the parched timbers with clear-drying oils restored the aged wood to its original warmth. Caramel sofas are by Summer Hill Ltd., Redwood City, California. Handmade *passementerie* from West Coast Trimmings embellishes the Cameron Collection ottoman. Leslie Hannon loop moss fringe frames pillows and the window treatment, while an iron chandelier from France, circa 1870, stakes claim to the airspace.

❧ Wait for the hostess to unfold her napkin and place it in her lap before doing so.

❧ In a country where dining has been elevated to art, it is proper to gently fill a soup spoon at the bowl's nearest edge by sweeping the spoon toward the body then up to the mouth and sipping from the point. (Slurping one's soup as well as tipping one's bowl are capital offenses.) No matter that on this side of the Atlantic it is correct to scoop the spoon away from the body and sip from the side.

❧ The first time the main course is offered, take a small serving, as it will be passed a second time. Besides, theoretically, one should finish the food on one's plate. At a formal dinner the salad, cheese and dessert are not passed again, nor, of course, is the *entrée*.

❧ Though doing so may prove challenging, hold the knife in the right hand and the fork in the left with the tines pointed down. It is poor form to transfer the utensils back and forth. Until the mid-nineteenth century, people oceans apart ate with the fork in the right hand. But in 1853, soon after a French book of etiquette described the style favored by the most fashionable, nearly all Europeans began eating with the knife in the right hand and the fork in the left with the tines down.

Mixing elegance with ease warms an amply proportioned family room that works for enjoying the company of friends, playing board games with grandchildren and watching television. The latter hides in the majestic eighteenth-century *buffet deux corps* from Country French Interiors, Dallas.

RIGHT: Offering an element of surprise is a five-legged chair from Jacqueline Adams Antiques, Atlanta, that does not compromise on comfort. Fabric by Pierre Frey dresses the antique Louis XV *bergère*, while the Stark Carpet striped sisal introduces a casual touch.

LEFT: For obvious reasons, it is best to cull 19th-century hymnals—scratches and all —from a local resource rather than tote them from Paris's Porte de Vanves flea market a continent away.

FACING: During the holidays, a mantel becomes a strong focal point with garland, magnolia leaves and berries that not only create a verdant look but also add warmth at the coldest time of the year.

Obsessed with their pets, the French treat their canine companions like children, though, by all appearances, French children must follow rules that are more rigid. Although an ocean away, a pampered six-year-old Norwich terrier also gets the royal treatment with monogrammed linens and his own Patina bed. Yet his favorite place to loll is on a silk-covered ottoman.

❧ When taking a sip of mineral water or wine, place both the knife and fork in the resting position—five o'clock—with the fork crossed over the knife—and rest the free hand on the table.

❧ Between courses hands must rest on the table, not in one's lap. Since the French frequently use their hands when speaking, clasping and unclasping the hands during a lively conversation, it also is acceptable to rest elbows on the table. When the next course arrives, hands go back on the table, elbows off.

❧ Try a portion of every course. Unless allergic to a food being served, it is a *faux pas* not to do so. One may refuse oysters, also cheese, but that is about it. Hostesses do appreciate guests who try the latter. Regarding the former: with their sophisticated palates, the French are ardent consumers. Like *foie gras*, raw oysters are often central to the menu, though mostly at the end of the year. Still, a hostess will rarely serve them unless sure her guests like and appreciate them.

❧ A cheese platter usually includes one soft-ripened, one pressed cooked-curd, one veined and perhaps one goat's milk that any *fromager*, or maker and seller of French cheeses, would be proud to supply. All say cheese should be served at room temperature and tasted in increasing order of flavors, from the freshest and mildest to the most fermented or strongest, using a separate serving knife for each family of cheeses to avoid mixing flavors. In fine restaurants, cheeses served are generally arranged on the plate in the recommended eating order.

Sensuous red Edelman Leather injects a bit of pizzazz, warming a family room's neutral palette—as if aware of the trend to avoid enveloping a setting in beige. Caramel, mushroom, coffee, cocoa, cappuccino, sand—yes. Greige—Parisian gray mixed with beige—definitely. Ruching *à la* a Prada handbag gives the throw pillow—and Hamilton chair—an unmistakable edge.

In 1615, fourteen-year-old princess Anne of Austria introduced chocolate to the French court upon marrying Louis XIII. Following her predecessor's example, Marie-Thérèse of Austria gave the future Louis XIV chocolate as an engagement gift, proclaiming she had merely two passions: the king and chocolate. This prompted the Sun King to appoint a royal chocolate maker; however, he did not dismiss his numerous mistresses.

✤ When taking a serving of cheese, it is important to preserve the shape, as the flavor varies from the rind to the heart. Simply slice a sliver of Brie or Roquefort, for example, along the wide side of the wedge, leaving the point and rounded back for all to share. Never cut the point off a wedge; it is a transgression to do so. Sample two or three different varieties—transferring each onto the cheese plate with the individual cheese knife, then transferring each onto a piece of bread. Never spread the cheese; just place it on a morsel of bread, pressing a little if afraid it will fall. It is improper to use a fork or the fingers to eat cheese.

✤ Nor is it proper to take a bite out of the whole piece of bread. Instead, tear a bite-size piece before eating.

✤ If asked to pass the salt, pass only the salt, not the salt and pepper. Here, the two are inseparable but not in France. Since salt has superstitious connotations, place it within easy reach rather than handing it directly to the person.

✤ Do not cut the salad; fold a leaf with the fork or the help of a small piece of bread. It is rare that leaves are large or unwieldy, since most hostesses see to that.

✤ Some Parisians say it is a supreme compliment to the hostess for a guest ask for a recipe; but do so later, not at the table.

Setting the bar is one with the same curving silhouette in the French capital's luxurious Hôtel Le Meurice—228, rue de Rivoli, (1st Arr.), across the street from Tuileries Gardens—that could rightfully boast of being the source of inspiration for this posh gathering spot where rich walnut panels and nineteenth-century Baccarat crystal chandeliers emit an inviting glow. Chic bar stools by Ebanista sit on 16-inch squares of honed chocolate brown and French refined light limestone flooring from Paris Ceramics USA, NYC. Ralph Lauren crystal, including champagne flutes, stand ready to serve Veuve Clicquot, a *négociant* wine—confirmed by the code NM on the label, meaning produced by one of the large houses that dominate the Champagne region of France. The letters RM on a label indicate that it is a grower's own wine, made with his own grapes. CM denotes a cooperative's wine.

Taking its name from a café located on the Place de la Bastille, is it any wonder this intimate meeting place exudes an old-world attitude? No matter that there is no wait staff scurrying from table to table, taking orders for chef-made soup and salad. In keeping with the French preference for rounded, tightly packed monochromatic arrangements, roses fresh from the flower market prop on Williams Sonoma's white hotel linens—cut to size then embroidered by design-minded Dallasite Joan Cecil.

In nineteenth-century France, bistros were popular spots where people with a passion for intellectualizing would congregate. Across from the bar here, family and friends alike socialize, parked side-by-side on a tufted banquette that Marroquin covered in Taffard fabric, or on Philippe Starck chairs at small cast-iron-and-marble-topped café tables beneath Baccarat pendant lights suspended from the high ceiling. Also Baccarat are the candlelit clear and black crystal *Ombres et Lumières,* shown above.

⚜ Always use a fork when eating *pommes frites* (French fries) or risk drawing curious stares. Fact is, the French eat most everything with a fork and knife or a fork and spoon, including pizza, bacon, asparagus and many sandwiches. It may be the ultimate in snobbery, but even a fresh-churned ice cream creation is generally served with a fork, though a hostess may also provide a spoon.

⚜ Men always pour the mineral water and the wine. Rather than refusing the latter, leave the glass full. Or a simple "*non merci*" will also suffice. Never cover the glass. If a woman would like more water, it is permissible for her to ask a man, but she must not ask that he refill her wine glass unless among good friends. Well-brought-up men know it is their role to keep an eye on a woman's wine glass, the thinking goes.

⚜ It is very, very, very bad form ever to leave the dinner table. Unless there is a genuine emergency, the timing could not be worse. In that case, fold the napkin in half and set it to the left of the plate, not on the chair.

⚜ And something else: it is unacceptable to apply lipstick at the table. In fact, it simply is NOT done. French women are united in the belief that "a woman must never put on lipstick in public; one does that in private." It is part of a woman's "*toilette*." "She must never let anyone witness her grooming in public."

❧ Following dessert, the host will stand and invite guests into the salon. Place the napkin—unfolded—on the table to the right of the plate, with the knife and fork uncrossed on the plate. Do not offer to help clear the table. But do push the chair toward the table.

❧ The French always serve coffee and liqueurs in the salon, since most, quite naturally, have one. What's more, there are chairs for everyone and *gigognes,* (small, moveable nesting tables) for the exclusive purpose of placing cups and drinks. Indeed, whether dissecting the workings of their nation or more commonplace issues, discussions must continue after the meal, even after a lingering one followed by dessert. For one to simply pick up and leave without engaging in further conversation—at one's intellectual best—is not an option, as doing so constitutes an affront.

❧ Another well-established habit that has not dimmed with age: around an hour after midnight, the serving of fresh-squeezed orange juice signals that coffee and alcohol service has ended for the night. Shortly thereafter, it is permissible to make a graceful exit. If one happens to be spending the night, it might help to know that upon leaving it is tradition to tip *domestiques,* or help, acknowledging that one's presence has inevitably created added work.

❧ Afterwards, be sure to send a handwritten thank-you note, never abbreviating Madame, Monsieur or Mademoiselle, lest your hosts think you are rude.

For reasons that are clear, when dining in Paris, it is wise to do as the Parisians do rather than risk unknowingly raising their well-groomed eyebrows, or even offending them. But more notably, an invitation to dine in a French home is indeed a distinct privilege. It is not often that the French open their homes to acquaintances. To increase one's chances of being invited again, it helps to demonstrate one's understanding of the French culture as a means of expressing one's desire to have a place in their highly structured world.

ABOVE: In contrast to other cultures, the French set their tables with the fork tines facing down—a custom some say developed to undercut the fork's ability to snag ruffled lace sleeves and cuffs. Others claim someone thought the tines of forks and bowls of spoons looked less aggressive face down, saying nothing about drawing attention to engraved initials or the decorative motifs without being obvious. In fairness, the flip sides liberally borrow flourishes from various chapters of French history and often are even more decorative.

LEFT: Many credit the formidable Catherine de Médici (1519–89), who came to Paris in 1533 at age 14 to wed the future King Henri II (1519–59), with defining acceptable table manners. Educated in Florentine mores, she brought along an entourage of Italian chefs and pastry cooks, in addition to the dozens of silver dinner forks packed in her luggage. And, yet, Louis XIV (1643–1715) was the first French monarch to offer guests three-piece place settings of a knife, fork and spoon, though he chose to eat with his fingers throughout his life, even at elaborate *fêtes*.

THE FINE ART OF LESS

For some, it seems, the sky may be the limit when creating an international air—and that is their God-given right. But when Mies van der Rohe (1886–1969), the visionary German architect, said, "Less is more," he surely was not taking issue with putting on the Ritz with lavish displays of wealth and power as a way of promoting one's self-image or wowing others. Actually, what he said was not about money at all, nor was he championing spare, minimalist living. Seeing possibilities in creating open, free-flowing spaces drew him to the challenge of designing an advanced structural ideal with minimal framework. No matter. Lately, it seems, his message has been taken to heart.

With overindulgence no longer having a place among twenty-first-century economic worries, less—or certainly far less lofty—is now plenty inside many stateside spaces. In a notable shift, a more conservative way of life is emerging, in keeping with the new national mood. As if acknowledging that there are concerns more serious these days than hiring a personal trainer, buying a flashy car, or even taking a costly vacation to Europe, South America or Asia, spare elegance warms interiors, pleasing without overwhelming. This is not to suggest that economic realities alone

Rather than the expected chair and table, a subtly curved sofa by Marroquin Upholstery, Dallas, strewn with pillows fits comfortably—and perfectly—in a stairwell bedecked in Scalamandré. A shimmery fabric from Allan Knight skims the table, embellished with a Houlès trim that joins a Bergamo textile. The Cortina floor lamp with white gold leaf finish is from Palmer Designs, La Jolla, California. A collection of old mirrors, gathered over time on shopping forays in France, reflects the setting. The sterling silver tea set is by Buccellati.

sparked the growing mind-set reflecting the influence of deeply conservative France—a country that abolished its extravagant ways more than three hundred years ago—where it has long been unacceptable to flaunt material possessions that are showy symbols of wealth, or, more precisely, draw attention to dissimilar economic means.

Book-worthy testaments to aesthetic visions and glossy monthly magazines that land at our doors also deserve credit for encouraging minimalist attitudes. Delivering interiors stripped of excess flourishes, settings tout classic style from a present-day point of view—aided, of course, by tastemakers with discerning eyes, savvy skills and fresh, edgy ideas. Together they are kindling growing excitement in less materialistic, more conservative, value-conscious principles. Indeed, how else to explain the French *art de vivre* now prompting us to live with less, considering that less has seldom really seemed like an acceptable option to a people with a penchant for the finer things in life?

Elegant petit fours from Dallas Affaires Cake Company taste every bit as divine as an assortment of tiny *macarons* from high-end French *pâtisseries* such as Ladurée, Fauchon and Pierre Hermé. The *macaron* (from the Italian *maccherone* and the Venetian *macarone*, meaning "fine paste" and pronounced *mack-ah-rohn* in France, not mack-a-roon as in English,) has been a mainstay of French pastry since Queen Catherine de Medici, Henri II's wife, introduced the Florentine delicacy in the mid-sixteenth century.

FACING: A middle staircase is wrapped in beauty from Iron Age Studios. Lantern from Ainsworth-Noah, Atlanta, is old.

Once poised in the shadow of larger commodes at the Paris flea market, a Louis XV petite commode, or *chiffonnière*—literally, French for "rag picker," intended to hold miscellaneous items in its four small drawers—now has a place of honor beneath *Paris on a Rainy Day* by Etienne-Albert Eugene Joannon (1857–1910). France remains true to blue or *tendre gris*, the ever-present color morphing between gray, green and blue, depending on the light and the season. In the states, look to Houston-based antiques dealer Joyce Horn for furnishings in a similar hue.

Adding global style to the grandeur of the entry hall is a set of architectural watercolors of the Louvre by Dallas artist Daniel Heath (www.heathwatercolors.com). The world's most famous art museum, built late in the twelfth century, served as one of numerous royal residences for nearly seven hundred years. Louis XIV resided at the *Palais du Louvre* before moving his court to Versailles in 1678. In 1793, the Louvre became a museum.

Tiebacks with bold glass beads are from the Paris flea market.

LEFT: Artistic Frame canopy chairs with a flattering silhouette command attention in a reading nook draped in silks by Jim Thompson and Sanderson. The French rock-crystal chandelier, circa 1840, is from Marvin Alexander, NYC, and the intense coral throw is by D. Porthault. Even the recession didn't curtail a yearning for irresistible Emily, a monkey with a taste for beignets and mischief. *Emily Goes Wild* is by author Betty Lou Phillips.

Down the hall from the master bedroom stands a *lingerie*, or linen room, permeating the air with the fresh scent of laundry water from Edith Mézard, an authority on French linens. Those at her Château de l'Ange, in Lumières, Provence, often wear a single embroidered word, such as *bonheur (happiness), amour* or *simple*. Early *châteaux* often had a spacious area for storing large quantities of household *linges* (linens), suiting the rhythms of daily life—sleeping, bathing and eating—since, in some, laundering occurred only twice a year.

FACING: Upscale stylishness extends into the laundry, where Belgian lace tops the Ralph Lauren cotton lining baskets. Today well-dressed beds demand freshly ironed linens, even in households pressed for time. An appliance known as a mangle in our parents' era and now called a rotary iron takes a New York minute to deliver a crisply pressed sheet.

Energy-efficient washers and dryers put an exhilarating spin on a laundry, while Stark Wallcovering's pale pink vinyl—resembling patent leather, though, of course, it will not wrinkle or crack—lifts the gloom of washday.

A bead board drying rack from Ballard Designs holds hand washables from Hip, Hip Hooray, Dallas.

With laundry rooms coming up from basements and leaving behind exposed pipes, ceilings are aiming higher too. Here, crowning touches include a pair of shabby-chic chandeliers from I Lite 4 U, Santa Ana, California, and a lacy-looking ceiling so delicate that it resembles plasterwork, courtesy Sanders Studio, Dallas.

"No accessory is too unimportant to consider," wrote Dorothy Draper, who established in 1923 the first interior design company in the United States. Though not a coin laundry, a bank hosts money left in pockets or found in the bottom of the washer. Family tradition holds that residents divide the holdings once a year.

Clothespin hardware from River Ridge, Inc. in Waco, Texas, dresses a laundry for success while adding a bit of fun.

PAST PERFECT

It is fair to say that to this day the eighteenth century is thought the most elegant era in European history, with period-perfect French furniture justly singled out for praise. Of course, with its diverse regional variety, the furnishings of Louis XIV, Louis XV and Louis XVI can take many forms—some more ornately embellished than most loyal aficionados might choose, others in step with current moods and attitudes.

At the century's beginning, when Louis XIV ruled France from the glorious Palace of Versailles, the king's *maître ébéniste* (chief cabinetmaker), André-Charles Boulle (1642–1732), laboriously fashioned the finest woods into regal inlaid furniture, baroque in its elaborateness. As if exhibiting proof of the court's unassailable wealth and authority, intricate ivory, tortoiseshell and brass, or mother-of-pearl veneered into marquetry patterns exaggerated the beauty of each piece. Rich ormolu, or gilded bronze moldings and medallions, also offered bold standards for royal palaces throughout Europe, while enticing the French aristocracy to mirror the king's extravagances. >114

"The bed has become a place of luxury for me," Napoléon once said, surely aware that during the reign of Louis XIV plank platforms supported mattresses stuffed with leaves, straw and pine needles. Inviting admiration: a hand-painted Patina bed impeccably dressed in Frette linens, a D. Porthault throw and bolts of fabric by Fortuny, the elegant Italian textile company that first captivated the upper classes on the eve of World War II. Faded Oriental rug is from Stark Carpet. Bombé Veneto chest is by Patina. And, yes, a Royal-Pedic mattress set is fit for an emperor—or empress.

The origin of painted furniture can be traced to the ancient Egyptian sarcophagus. Its popularity grew, however, in late-seventeenth-century France, when Louis XIV received a small red lacquered Japanese table from the Ambassador of Siam. Posh gray hand-finished Venetian plaster befits a bedroom that is the ultimate retreat. But, then, "The color of Paris is gray," the couturier Karl Lagerfeld observed, undoubtedly aware that in the winter gray clouds hover in the sky.

FACING: Back in the eighteenth century, the bedroom was where high-level meetings took place— until Madame de Pompadour removed her *chambre* from the list of public rooms. To this day, the French subscribe to the separation of public and private places, keeping bedroom doors tightly closed, feeling it is the most personal of spaces. The eighteenth-century Louis XV–period limestone *cheminée* is from Saintes, on the western coast of France. Muscari, more commonly known as purple hyacinths, grace the fireplace. Although roses were Marie Antoinette's favorite flower, she also favored hyacinths.

Befitting the snobbery of Louis XIV's court, protocol dictated on which type sheeting—pure linen, a mix of linen and cotton, or pure cotton—one would sprawl. Nowadays, of course, fine linens are no longer the domain of the rich and noble.

LEFT: Deep carving, a shaped bonnet and the patina of age—the distinctive luster resulting from centuries of exposure to heat, humidity and light, to say nothing of oil from loving hands—add to an armoire's worth. Piercing, hardware and palatial size can also add value.

BELOW: Leading to the master bedroom is Vervolet hardware, made in Belgium for E. R. Butler & Co. French architect Hector Guimard, known for designing the Art Nouveau signage for the Paris Métro's entrances, was among the prominent Vervolet designers responsible for creating a daunting selection.

RIGHT: At the Petit Trianon, the small *château* that became Marie Antoinette's private domain at Versailles, she could escape the rigid, stifling formality of court life. Mirrored panels, mechanically raised from the floorboards, covered the windows, reflecting the candlelight in her boudoir on overnight stays. By day, the panels remained hidden in the flooring—an inventiveness unique to the age. Fabric shown is by J. Robert Scott. Trim is from Janet Yonaty.

It is standing room only at a coffee bar tucked into a niche on HER side of the bathroom. France's oldest coffeehouse, if not the oldest in the world, is Café Procope, founded in 1686 at 13 rue de l'Ancienne-Comédie 75006 Paris. With its marble tables, crystal chandeliers and walls lined in mirrors, not to mention its elegant silver coffee pots, it set the standard for Parisian cafés.

One needed a title, however, to appreciate the majesty of the tall, ostentatious chairs with upholstered, haughty-looking backs and stretchers reinforcing the legs. Since only the self-indulgent king was allowed to sit in a *fauteuil*, or armchair, there was an abundance of lowly stools and benches—all covered in regal fabrics, including embroidered silk. Shimmering brocades opulently threaded with gold, exquisite damasks and sumptuous velvets garnished with handmade silk *passementerie* radiated elegance *nonpareil*. Famed Gobelin tapestries made in Paris and carpets from Aubusson, Beauvais and the merged Savonnerie and Gobelin factories added layers of splendor to rooms.

Late in the seventeenth century, small rooms designed for grooming—*les toilettes*, meaning both dressing rooms (*cabinets de toilette*) and the toilet itself—appeared. Here, a nineteenth-century silvered French chandelier drenched in crystals gives HER marble bathroom instant panache.

When Louis XIV died in 1715, his five-year-old great-grandson became King Louis XV (1710–74). Accordingly, the king's uncle, Philippe II, the Duke of Orléans, was appointed regent, or temporary governor of France, until his nephew attained legal majority in February 1723. The transitional period—between the opulent baroque style associated with the Sun King and the less formal rococo look of Louis XV—became known as Régence.

ABOVE: European elegance drips from Sherle Wagner rock crystal fittings into the firm's china sink.

FACING: Centuries ago, Emperor Napoléon III's bejeweled Empress Eugénie's interest led to a rage for alluring perfume bottles. Today, factices—factitious, artificial bottles that serve as prototypes for perfumeries—are collectible. A vintage tiered cake stand holds face cloths and bath salts. Adding further splendor to HER bathroom are a pair of silver gilt wall lamps by Vaughn, a nineteenth-century French chandelier from Jacqueline Adams, Atlanta, and artful Venetian plaster walls by Southwest Progressive, Dallas.

Artisans used oak for the finest pieces, pine and poplar for ones more ordinary, ushering in less-imposing furniture with softened rigidity. Gentle curves and refined flourishes adorned the upper sections of armoires and other case pieces designed as storage, while shapely legs replaced straight ones. To accommodate petticoats, elbow rests on chairs were set farther back. Rather than resting on his laurels, *ébéniste* Charles Cressent placed *espagnolettes*—or female busts—at the corners of flat-top desks, chests of drawers and console tables.

Much like at an *haute* getaway that renews the spirit, a long, narrow soaking tub marries luxury and purpose. Hand carved in Italy from a single piece of Carrara marble, the smoothly honed tub is from Urban Archaeology, NYC. (Michelangelo's famous sculpture, *David*, is also made of Carrara marble.) Warm bath sheets are courtesy of Myson, manufacturer of towel warmers for resort spas.

FACING: Rows of rhinestones from M & J Trimmings, NYC, embellish a slipcovered bath stool sporting multiple bows. During Louis XIV's reign, it was the men, not the women, who wore bows—on their sleeves, shoes, collars. And though resources often credit Louis XV with adding plumbing to Versailles, Louis XIV, rather than his wife, had the first *cabinet des bains*, or bathing room—filled with two marble tubs.

Furthermore, a fascination increased with the Far East that began in 1670, when the Trianon de Porcelaine at Versailles was built for one of Louis XIV's mistresses. When demand for all things Asian—from silk screens and lacquered cabinets with gleaming varnished finishes to blue-and-white porcelain vases and embroidered hangings—outstripped supply, French craftsmen copied these richly decorated pieces, then added showy flourishes of their own. The look brought together Far Eastern inspiration and Western artisanship, creating the foundation for the style now known as chinoiserie.

A brushed nickel Sherle Wagner lever rocks. Pure quartz, called rock crystal, is colorless and popular.

The Régence era pointed the way for the more beguiling rococo period (1730 to 1760) when Louis XV and his official mistress, or *maîtresse en titre*, Madame de Pompadour, had great influence on the decorative arts. Though public reception rooms retained their glamour and grandeur, the former Jeanne-Antoinette Poisson refashioned family apartments into less-formal settings, where the pastels she favored replaced strong colors. With a new reserve embracing comfort, she sought inviting chairs rather than stools, and fluid furniture arrangements conducive to conversation.

FACING: Chests draped in cloth served as dressing tables until early in the eighteenth century, when *tables de toilette*, known also as *poudreuses*, made their debut equipped with mirrored lids. Regardless that the drawers of Madame de Pompadour's multiple dressing tables held grandiose collections of brushes, perfumes and *pommades*, or face creams. Surely, she would have coveted this rhinestone-tufted vanity stool fashionably dressed in fabric from Lelièvre, Paris. The rhinestone tape is available from M & J Trimmings, NYC. The Art Déco lamps are from the Paris flea market.

In Paris, where appearance means a lot, mirror-lined closet doors and striking hardware befit suites within the grand Hôtel de Crillon, one of the capital's six palace hotels. In tribute to the artistry of the French, a stateside dressing room embraces upholstery from John Derian, NYC, dressed in Rubelli, Zimmer + Rohde and Ralph Lauren fabrics. *Très chic* tables are by Murray's Iron Works, and *haute joaillerie* (jewelry) for the closet—rock crystal knobs, garland pulls and Renaissance hinges—is from Sherle Wagner International.

FACING: Behind closed doors, high fashion marries luxury and purpose, reflecting more than a little uptown glam. Glazing lends an old-world aura to metallic finishes edging antiqued mirror-lined drawers. Crystal lamp from Brunschwig & Fils wears a shapely shade by Cele Johnson, Dallas. Sumptuous shag area rug is from Stark Carpet.

A setting with ample space for lounging and dressing also has plenty of room for an inspiration board that complements the metallic palette. Here, notes and cards from family and friends have a place of honor.

OPPOSITE, ABOVE: Dazzling, exquisitely crafted Sherle Wagner pulls add to the setting's romantic allure.

OPPOSITE, BELOW: Never mind that life has its more than occasional hiccups: this tip from Collette has the power to make one focus on its bright sides.

As a result, the king's highly skilled *menuisier* (chair maker), Jean-Baptiste Tilliard (1686–1766), sculpted a perfectly proportioned, low, curved armchair with an exposed-wood frame but without the stretcher or crosspiece seen on previous chairs. On the seat rail of the *bergère*, he carved a basket of flowers. On its back, he shaped shells and *cartouches*, or fanciful scrolls, communicating that rather than line the wall, this chair was to be moved about, making intimate conversation effortless.

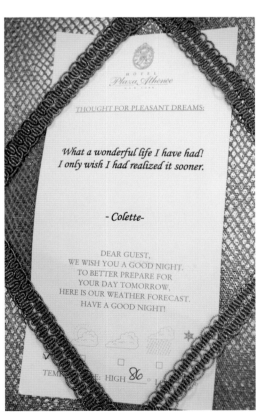

As Parisian chair makers began adopting Tillard's designs, the frames of both caned and Louis XV *bergère* chairs were at times gilded or painted. Upholstered arms were moved back from the length of the seat so fashionable crinolines would not be crushed. When hoop skirts were no longer in vogue, they would again extend forward, but soft, loose pillows still rested on fabric-covered platforms and curvaceous legs remained stretcher-free. Even centuries later, the rich damasks and velvets favored for upholstery would be viewed as the height of chic. Meanwhile, the *chaise longue* (literally, long chair) emerged as a *tour de force* that Western taste would come to behold, followed by the *escritoire*, a small desk with drawers and cubicles, also called a *secrétaire*.

Painstaking carvings on many wood pieces were pulled from all facets of nature, including shells, fish, waves, birds, vines, flowers, rocks and serpents. Also, designs were commonly rooted in farming motifs such as corn and wheat. Ribbons with streamers and hearts became fashionable too.

Dwellings in Paris flaunted brilliant crystal chandeliers and small, exquisitely carved marble mantels with large mirror panels, or painted overmantels called *trumeaux*. Wood floors boasted marquetry patterns, Versailles-like parquet designs often laid with alluring Aubusson or Savonnerie rugs. Whereas baroque style exuded a passion for symmetry, firmly holding that any chair, room or *château* divided vertically should be a precise mirrored-image half, rococo once again endorsed the asymmetry born in the Régence era.

Not everyone in France, however, was sold on grandeur and gloss. Many people preferred the unpretentious beauty of pieces produced outside Paris in woods echoing surrounding regions. If not quite astounding, armories and commodes were sufficiently commanding—generously scaled, graceful and easily identified by intricately carved decorative panels with exacting motifs. Eagles, flower baskets and garden instruments, for instance, were favored ornamentation in Lyon, Arles and Nimes, respectively, where artisans constructed furniture in sturdy walnut.

Rich mahogany paneling and Waterworks' gleaming Nero Marquina marble gives HIS bathroom a tailored, gentleman's club look—with radiant heated flooring and a heated towel warmer adding a bit of grandeur. The china sink is from Sherle Wagner.

Others opted for the unassuming splendor of neoclassical style, with straight, slender tapered legs and precise geometric shapes arranged symmetrically. Borrowing delicate motifs from ancient Greece and Italy's excavations of Pompeii and nearby Herculaneum, a desire for quiet sophistication shaped furnishings. As simplicity replaced excess, interiors appeared effortlessly elegant: color tones lightened, ceilings remained plain rather than frescoed, and no longer were wall panels profusely carved. Although the fresh beauty of neoclassical style first enchanted Madame de Pompadour and her brother, the Marquis de Marigny, in the late 1750s, decades before the death of Louis XV, it became increasingly popular during the reign of Louis XVI (1774–89).

To be sure, neoclassical leanings did not imply that Louis XV furniture had lost appeal—only that interest in the splendor of high-minded Louis XIV furnishings was dwindling. To this day, both Louis XV and Louis XVI pieces have the power of making the heart skip a beat, connecting with a refined mix of individuals, not just a cross-section of society.

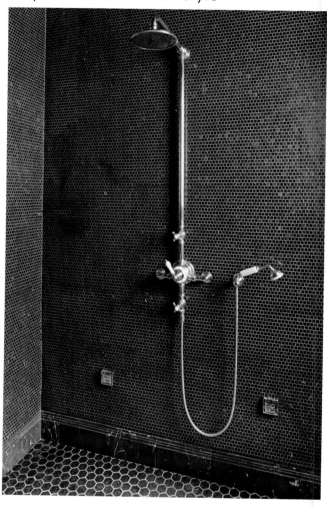

Both the marble lining the walls and the thermostatic wall valve trim is from the luxury bathroom company Waterworks.

FACING: An ample-sized shower, tiled in black marble, is fitted with distinctive features: a porthole window, slab bench—and a dog-friendly shower (unseen) with integrated hand shower and body spray.

There is no question that eighteenth-century furniture exerts a strong pull on those living an ocean apart, or that, quite naturally, the French bemoan seeing their precious heirlooms—near-perfect commodes, cherished armoires and beloved tables—with one-way tickets to cities in the United States, Canada or elsewhere in the world. Though periods other than the eighteenth century shape stateside dreams, the French view their fine French furnishings in the hands of shipping agents arranging overseas crossings as a step in the decline of their country's cultural heritage, a proud heritage they long to preserve and pass on to their children.

ABOVE: In Paris, the restoration of seriously dated interiors is routine, so for antique-style hardware the French often head to the *sous-sol*, or basement level of BHV—the spacious department store on the Rue de Rivoli near City Hall. The Bazar de l'Hotel de Ville, familiarly known locally as simply BHV, opened in 1856 when Baron Haussmann was modernizing Paris. The brass hardware shown here is from E. R. Butler, NYC.

FACING: HIS mahogany paneled dressing room is sensible as well as serviceable—and readily accessible from HIS bathroom.

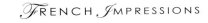

Exclusive, yes, and an ideal spot for perfecting one's putt. However, the illusion of a scenic view is deceiving, as Dallas artist Gillian Bradshaw-Smith tampers with perceptions. The synthetic green, rough and cart path are from Southwest Greens, Fort Worth.

Unlike most private clubs, there are no rules specifying who can and cannot enter this Men's Locker Room—but, then, nothing here is quite what it appears at first sight.

A door opens to a no-frills storage space, lacking the usual paraphernalia a pro shop generally stocks. *Trompe l'oeil,* an artistic style rooted in ancient Rome, is French for "tricks the eye."

Noble Pursuits

For those with means, shopping was a noble pastime in eighteenth-century France, especially along the tony rue du Faubourg Saint-Honoré, where *marchands-merciers*, or dealers in works of fine art, furniture and antiques, played a visible role in *décoration intérieure*, that is, interior decoration. Prohibited by guild rules from making case goods themselves, deft luxury goods merchants instead conceptualized and then commissioned *ébénistes* to construct masterfully assorted furnishings explicitly for the rooms where they would dwell.

One hundred years after a major flood swept through Paris, causing widespread damage, rain still cannot dampen the ardor of shoppers. Standing out from the crowd is an umbrella from Joie de Vivre, Modesto, California, printed with images of the Eiffel Tower and the Pont-Neuf, the capital's oldest bridge.

Among the notable clientele of the highly respected *marchand-mercier* Lazare Duvaux (1703–58) were King Louis XV and Madame de Pompadour (1721–64), whose persuasive force was behind pushing the king to move his court from Versailles to Paris and permitting nobles to live in their own houses.

No matter that, in keeping with royal whims, an entourage typically moved the king's prized possessions from one sumptuous domicile to the next, installing the furnishings wherever the king and his admirers went. In the mind of Madame de Pompadour, Paris demanded refined, shapelier silhouettes befitting living areas more modestly scaled than the vast, lofty spaces of Versailles. So, emboldened by her position, she took it upon herself to replace the heroic-proportioned, baroque ceremonial furniture of Louis XIV, the king's great-grandfather, and influence the period's fine and decorative arts.

In a revolt against earlier taste, she patronized the top *marchands-merciers,* seeking elegantly scaled, gracefully curved chairs and *canapés* (settees) outlined in flawlessly carved exposed wood frames. Then she ordered that seating float rather than line the walls to make intimate conversations less challenging. As mistress of the house, her authority was uncontested, which is not to say that members of the court welcomed taking orders from a commoner—especially one resented most deeply and talked about in a less-than-flattering light. (Plainly, the people of France railed against the taxes required to pay for her lavish extravagance, fueling decades-long grudges.)

ABOVE: The best down comes from geese that live in the coldest climates—Siberia, for example.

FACING: Rich, gratifying and highly addictive, chocolate reigns. Paired with Pierre Frey's white *matelassé*, it becomes even more enticing. Nonetheless, a steel bed from Michael Shannon & Associates, San Francisco, turns out to be the focal point. Neiman Marcus's Signoria Firenze's tailored, 400-thread count, Egyptian-cotton linens hide under Yves DeLorme's plump goose-down pillows and comforter. A choice of pillows—firm for those who sleep on their side, medium for back sleepers and soft for stomach sleepers—assure that guests rest in comfort and style. Luggage sports the globally recognized Louis Vuitton motif. Striped area rug is from Stark Carpet.

While some dealers failed to recognize the influence Madame de Pompadour wielded over the king, Lazare Duvaux wisely shared her goals. Soon, exquisitely crafted functional furnishings took up fractions of the space that Louis XIV pieces occupied. *Secrétaires*, writing tables, powdering tables, small gaming tables—created for cards or backgammon—reading stands, commodes and *chiffonnières* all debuted boasting curvaceous cabriolet legs.

In Victorian times, a writing table was a must-have in the bedroom. Today, it serves as another hotel-like amenity, offering guests a fitting spot to check their e-mail, peruse the morning paper or spread out work-related papers while savoring an early morning *café au lait*. An unassuming brown-and-white check from Bengal House robes a Hamilton chair.

RIGHT: There is no dashing out to get the morning papers or pick up faxes that have arrived during the night. Instead, one feels like an honored guest indeed.

FACING: In a snug corner of a room with all the accoutrements of a five-star hotel, fabric from Brunschwig & Fils clads a chaise by Summer Hill Ltd. With a raised pattern that resembles quilting, refreshing white *matelassé*—in French, meaning to cushion or pad—serves as a backdrop for a vintage bar cart, which works as a book table.

GOOD MORNING

To be sure, many pieces still tended to be ornately embellished—inlaid with gilt-bronze mounts; however, Madame de Pompadour's unerring taste clearly set a new tone for more stylish living and decorating. In turn, artisans from across Europe settled in Paris in hope of providing furnishings to the court of Louis XV, the king's subjects and his official mistress, naturally.

Shapely lettering on classic napkin rings purchased in the City of Light inspired both the choice of words and the script on inlaid tile rugs, and on towels too—illustrating that details do make a significant difference. In France, it is proper to address all women who have completed their education, married or not, as Madame rather than Mademoiselle. What's more, it is inappropriate to greet anyone French by simply saying, "Bonjour," without adding Madame, Monsieur or Mademoiselle.

Together with Duvaux she transformed cold, ceremonial rooms into more intimate, comfortable spaces that were use-specific. In time, all royal residences boasted numerous salons (*petit salon*, *salon de compagnie*, *salon de musique*) and a library, or *cabinet à écrire*. Each imperial bedroom had its own *garde-robe*, or dressing room and *boudoir*, a place to pout when not serving as a reception room. >158

FACING: With gray polished marble seemingly an indispensable backdrop in the French capital's grandest hotel bathrooms, Waterworks' Carrara marble freestanding metal-leg washstands, matte nickel sinks and fittings that read *chaud* (hot) and *froid* (cold) more than hint of Parisian glamour, as do sconces wearing Cele Johnson shades.

A tiered shelf is not just decorative; it hosts most everything one needs to indulge the senses.

FACING: In a bathroom with modern amenities, Waterworks' freestanding "Candide" tub, cast in iron, bathes guests in luxury, while a vintage pharmacy chest with industrial simplicity adds to its charm.

LEFT: Lending a nod to former French colonies in Africa, artifacts from the Ivory Coast, or Senegal, for example, have long embellished homes of the well traveled. Tame by comparison, a family-friendly stateside setting makes a bold statement with faux-leather walls and Cameron Collection chairs decked in Scalamandré's graphic zebra linen. Oak floors are hand-scraped.

RIGHT: Chess is not only challenging but also fun when sleek cut-out profiles form words defining the roles various pieces play. The black-and-white set elevated to an art form was made in Italy for Bergdorf Goodman, NYC.

FACING: Not exactly, the call of the wild, but a civilized place inspired by the lure of Africa guarantees to make one smile while playing chess, relaxing or watching a P.G.A. event or the BCS game on television. Fabrics are by Travers and Glant. St. Germain woven trunks from Ralph Lauren serve as tables.

An antique partner's desk (unseen) and aged leather chairs from Ralph Lauren present an argument for working in comfort at home. The Cape Lodge trunk, hurricane lamps and wicker tray also are by Ralph Lauren, infusing the setting with the spirit of South Africa. The Hartmann zebra rug was a gift. The largest of the mountain zebras, the species appear whiter than Cape mountain zebras, since their black stripes are narrower and more widely spaced.

FACING: Today's thirst for leather dates back to the 1920s, when Parisian designer Jean-Michael Frank first obtained skins from the revered Hermés for use in furniture making. Oak floors are hand-scraped. When not at war, Napoléon traveled with a library of books, including volumes on religion, history and poetry, plus some novels.

Brass sink and fittings are from Waterworks. Bar top is Tobacco Croc Matouche, made in Italy for Walker Zanger.

FACING: Behind the closet door dwells Ralph Lauren's leopard wall covering. A few well-chosen pieces—on hangers that have been hand painted—plus a touch of style and the right attitude are all it takes to be casually cool when walking on the wild side.

As if borrowing the title page from American writer Maurice Sendak's classic children's book *Where the Wild Things Are*, a hallway sets the stage for a nearby bedroom. Binoculars—perfect for zooming in on animals handcrafted by Steiff, the famous German toy company that has been putting a gold button in one ear for more than 100 years—perch on an old French trunk from Ainsworth-Noah, Atlanta. Photographs—a gift—that capture the spirit of a family's African adventure nearly fill a wall, while clocks from Pottery Barn Kids confirm that decorating is not just about indulging wildly expensive tastes.

Deluxe accommodations befitting a luxury camp resort sport Scalamandré fabrics and five-star Porthault bed linens worthy of envy by anyone on an expedition. Clarence House burlap scales the walls, creating a natural backdrop. The shaggy-chic grass-green rug is from Stark Carpet. Other wild touches, including the animal print file folders, are from Ballard Designs catalog (ballard designs.com).

FACING: A Pierre Frey fabric with animal magnetism provides a guide to Africa's tourist-friendly Tanzania, Malawi, and Zambia. The vintage stove with a weight problem is from the Whimsey Shoppe, Dallas.

RIGHT: Branching out—in a room with 10-foot ceilings—a handcrafted chandelier by Deanna Wish Designs, New Castle, Pennsylvania, swings over the Ralph Lauren brass bed, boldly conveying a sense of adventure.

LEFT: For immediate relief of chocolate cravings, lovesickness, exam pressure, mild anxiety and extreme hunger, a dose of Emergency Chocolate sits ready. For the exotic designer chocolate infused with a delectable sense of humor go to www. bloomsberryusa.com. Those passionate about chocolate can also retrace the eventful 4,000-year history of cocoa at the Choco-Story in Paris. Opened in 2010, the museum—at 28 blvd Bonne Nouvelle, 10th Arr.—focuses on the origin and development of chocolate, along with various methods of making the coveted indulgence.

FACING: Obviously, it is a jungle in here, though the kind of spot where a young boy loves to bunk down. Big game hunters coined the phrase "the Big Five," referring to the lion, leopard, rhinoceros, elephant and Cape buffalo, the most dangerous and difficult animals to hunt on foot. Today, however, it is more common to use the term from the safety of a Land Rover—on a photographic safari—or simply surround oneself with wild animal patterns. Schumacher's giraffe linen outfits a Summer Hill chair. Cut fringe on the seat cushion is from Leslie Hannon.

It is safe to say that, in return for his assistance, Lazare Duvaux won the enduring gratitude and respect of the king. For he was appointed *ébéniste du Roi* and accorded lodgings in the Gobelins, a royal establishment where he was immune to the rigid rules of the guild. When he moved to the Arsenal in 1756, he enjoyed the same privileges—and thus earned a place in the history of French furniture and the decorative arts.

Of perhaps more significance, however, much of what we know about aristocratic interiors during the reign of Louis XV can be credited to him. For a decade, beginning in 1748, he chronicled the names of his customers, along with minute details relating to their orders. His journal then sat in the Paris archives for more than a century after his death. In 1873, not long before fire destroyed the archives, it was published. From *marchand-mercier* Lazare Duvaux, it is possible to glimpse fragments of lives with a passion for refined eighteenth-century French furnishings, fragments that otherwise would remain unknown.

Confirming what we already knew: it helps if there's a first-aid station nearby when cuts, scrapes and scratches occur, whether on a jaunt in the wild or at home.

FACING: An environmentally friendly Hartmann & Forbes shade joins forces with an open-weave Calvin fabric to block the light yet allow a stream of cool air in on days when tracking animals at dawn is unappealing. The floor-skimming twine panels tumble from a basic rod wrapped in hardware-store rope.

Camping goes luxe with Waterworks' handmade copper French soaking tub, brass fittings and teak mat, not to mention floor-to-ceiling polished mahogany travertine from Walker Zanger, set on walls in a running bond pattern. Flooring is installed on the diagonal—with mosaic strips of Opus Anticato dark travertine separating the 16-inch by 16-inch squares. Size does matter. Nowadays, people are shunning the 12-inch by 12-inch tile known as the builder stock look.

FACING: Animal instincts move out of Africa and into a stateside bathroom with the trappings of the good life: tiger-striped Porthault towels, Waterworks hammered-copper sink and brass fittings. Sconces from Urban Archaeology, NYC, don ocelot-print shades (fabricated from a standard pillowcase) to keep watch over the custom washstand with ample towel storage. Dark, weathered leather frames the mirror.

LEFT: At Le Louvre Antiques, Dallas, the competition for attention is intense; yet, this humble *porte-journal* stood out among much grander finds. (*Hebdomadaires* means weeklies, but now the French use the word *publicités* for advertisements rather than *réclames*.) The piece is typical of the south of France, specifically the region near L'Isle-sur-la-Sorgue, the Lubéron's matchless center for antiques 25 kilometers southeast of Avignon.

BELOW: Recycled laundry bags find a home on this side of the Atlantic. They are from the Mews, Dallas, a stable of antiques shops.

FACING: Partial to purple, Marie Antoinette splashed private rooms in her favorite shades, washed wood pieces in dignified greenish gray and enveloped her Versailles boudoir with a toile de Jouy, which is French for cloth—and the name given to fabrics made at the Oberkampf factory in Jouy-en-Josas, the French town not far from the palace. Maps are of Paris.

Four full-size beds, unmistakably Patina with Venetian leanings, line a room set to pamper granddaughters. There are no blackout dates, of course, when cousins can meet. *De rigueur* testaments to the power of their Nana's love include in-house dining, laundry and turndown service, a wall-mounted flat-screen television and iPod docking stations. In addition, a promised trip to the nearby Tory Burch boutique helps guarantee repeat visits.

ABOVE: What nicer way to end the day than by knowing somebody loves you. "P.S. I Love You" is an edgy update on the more traditional "Sweet Dreams" and in keeping with the mood. Italian bedding from Schweitzer Linen, San Francisco, offers sufficient reason for sleeping in.

RIGHT: Fit for twenty-first century royalty—or granddaughters so enjoyable it's disarming—is a bed tray set with "Cafe Paris," from Bernardaud, the French porcelain company, and Neiman Marcus. Embroidered linens laud the Eiffel Tower.

ABOVE: A girly bedroom is both stunning and smart, dolled up in Bennison's "Lilac on Oyster," Manuel Canovas' "Cherubin," pale lavender walls and multicultural influences. Small details have a big way of making any room special.

BELOW: Ordinary white piqué shams and coverlets become extraordinary when monogrammed with each granddaughter's initials in spring green. Entwined lettering dates back to the ancient Egyptians; by the mid-sixteenth century, the taste had reached royal residences. Nowadays, though, bigger is better, and small is *passé*. What's more, the fonts used by Dallasite Joan Cecil are far from traditional.

RIGHT: Smocking—small, uniformly spaced gathers stitched decoratively into a honeycomb pattern—first appeared in thirteenth-century England as farmers found that outer garments, known as smocks, offered protection from the cold as well as freedom of movement. But the Industrial Revolution put a halt to the trend, as loose-fitting clothing required the wearer to move with care near machinery. Deep smocking then became more common on the clothing of women and children. From England, it spread to the Continent, then to the Americas, Australia, New Zealand and South Africa. Smocked window treatments and flat Roman shades (three unseen) are the work of Straight Stitch, Dallas. Stripe with the palest lavenders and greens is by Manuel Canovas. Check is from Kravet. Trim is by Houlès, Inc. Iron Age Studios, Dallas, fabricated the birds on a line.

LEFT: Spotless starched white linen mats —three unseen, all with the mixed message good night and good morning—put on the Ritz just like at the world-famous Ritz Hôtel in Paris (15, Place Vendôme). Designed by Hardouin-Mansart, the architect of Versailles, its exterior is a protected national landmark. Not stuffy, but certainly ritzy, the Ritz has been the place to see and be seen since opening its doors in 1898. Novelist Marcel Proust took inspiration from it. Coco Chanel called it her home for more than thirty years. The spirit of Ernest Hemingway flourishes. For royalty, business magnates, celebrities and visiting dignitaries, the palace remains a coveted address.

FACING: Inviting admiration is a fashion-forward half-borne, which is in the same family as a confidante—with numerous seats attached in a single unit—except slightly more sophisticated than its aristocratic counterpart. The find from Gallerie Marumo, Palm Beach, Florida, once adorned the country house of a nobleman living outside Paris. Fabric is from Robert Allen. Runner is from Stark Carpet.

Much like a boutique hotel, an *en suite* reading room offers wireless, high-speed Internet service, a modest stationery wardrobe and jars of M&M's and black licorice, appropriate considering the glossy black lacquer desktop surface. Lamps made in Italy exude an air of modernity bedecked in shades by Cele Johnson, Dallas. The walls reveal affection for family members. Ever since Louis XIV established the Royal Academy of Dance in 1661, professionals have trained aspiring ballet dancers.

Awash in clean lines and European influences, a bathroom with floor-to-ceiling marble makes a dramatic statement. The Waterworks' washstand with polished nickel bowls is custom. Oval tilted mirrors and wall sconces add even more pizzazz, while a separate shower with large showerhead (unseen) quiets the mind, soothes the senses and befriends the spirit in satisfying doses.

LEFT: A vintage pharmacy chest stocks items often forgotten when leaving home. It is also the perfect place for storing everything from towels to polish remover.

BELOW: Slipcovered in Rogers & Goffigan's white terry cloth, a bath stool gets personal. The words "Bare Necessities," embroidered in black, surround a sterling silver tray topped with soaps and lotions, much like at a full-service spa or at any of Paris's six palace hotels. When it opened in 1898, the Ritz led the way to guests wanting for nothing with bathtubs in rooms. Today heated towel bars also are common luxuries in French homes. The one here holds warm, thick towels from the Valombreuse boutique at 234 rue de Rivoli, between Paris's Hôtel de Crillon and Hôtel Le Meurice, across from the Louvre. As in France, the water closet has its own door, separating it from the rest of the bathroom.

RIGHT: Waffle-piqué robes and a hair dryer —hanging from a polished nickel hook—fit the room's designer wardrobe.

L'ATELIER

Simultaneously workshop, salon and instructional warren, the traditional French *atelier* has served some seven centuries as a creative sanctuary for continental artists and artisans.

These dens of inspiration can trace their origins to the *studiolo* of the Italian Renaissance—lavish retreats intended for study, contemplation, and the governance of private affairs. Set apart from the rest of the household, *studiolos* provided an intimate setting for aristocrats to attend to various tasks, from composing confidential correspondence and scrutinizing paperwork to hosting small gatherings of guests. In 1996, the Metropolitan Museum of Art painstakingly re-created the Studiolo Gubbio, commissioned by the Duke of Urbino in the fifteenth century. The sublime room with inlay-rich walls peered into upper-class Italian life, a nobility that extolled scholarship and artistic achievements above all other pursuits.

Esteemed Swiss-made Audemars Piguet wall clocks heighten the appeal of a side entrance, documenting time zones in Dallas, New York, London, Paris and Venice and connecting cultures. Meanwhile, three sets of 10-foot tall French doors welcome the late-afternoon sun.

In France, l'atelier became the artist's domain. Paul Cézanne (1839–1906), the stylistic genius who helped bridge Impressionism and modernism with his portfolio of vibrant landscapes, still lifes and portraits, built a studio near his childhood home of Aix-en-Provence. During the first decade of the twentieth century, the venerable painter schooled young artists in technique, while welcoming myriad colleagues to the modest rooms he designed himself. Nearly five decades after the master's death, Atelier Cézanne opened its doors to the public as a small museum. Since 1954, generations of visitors have enjoyed unrivaled proximity to his props, which include fruit bowls, a trio of human skulls, and one empty bottle of rum.

For American artist John Singer Sargent (1856–1925), *l'atelier* served as an essential refuge during the years following the disastrous debut of his infamous portrait *Madame X*. At one Parisian studio, Sargent painted a portrait of the landlady in lieu of paying rent, which he could scarcely afford after scathing reviews of his work drove away his commissions. The luminous *Madame Paul Poirson* currently resides at the Detroit Institute of Arts.

By no means were French *ateliers* the exclusive dominion of the fine artist. Milliners, embroiderers, seamstresses, carpenters, piano makers, ceramicists, gilders, goldsmiths, glassblowers, poets and playwrights all honed their talents and plied their trades in private workshops. Since the time of Marie Antoinette, haute couture has owed an indelible debt to skilled specialists. From catwalks to red carpets, the fruits of their labors set the standard for sartorial splendor. Today, the houses of Dior, Chanel, and Saint Laurent

54, rue du faubourg Saint Honoré, 8e

Until repurposed, an antique postal box welcomed the mail of residents living in one of the French capital's coveted *hôtel particuliers* converted to *appartements*. In its new life, it holds garage door openers, car keys, cell phones, dog brushes and more.

Menu du Jour

Asparagus Velouté

Slow Roasted Salmon with Sorrel Sauce

Noirmoutier Potatoes with Fleur del Sol

Parmesan Bread and Goat Cheese

Strawberry Orange Soup with Candied Lemon Zest

Miniature Lemon Tea Cakes

An espresso can offer the perfect afternoon break, or even take the edge off the need for a nap.

FACING: In Paris, long the uncontested capital of *haute* cuisine, most kitchens are small and many are tired looking, perhaps because they are more about cooking than socializing. Or it could be due to resistance to change from the time when they were servants' domains. Regardless, this well-equipped *atelier* kitchen appears fresh—with stainless steel appliances, soapstone countertops and graphic black-and-white marble flooring. All-Clad and Calphalon cookware from Williams-Sonoma insure the area is far from the servant's scullery of an earlier era.

Like design itself, an arrange-it-yourself clock from New York's Museum of Modern Art relies on juxtapositions, the harmonious balancing of color, texture and scale.

FACING: For nearly two centuries, the walled city of Calais, overlooking the Strait of Dover, has been synonymous with lace, exporting approximately three-fourths of its output to 140 countries. The port near the Belgium border now boasts *Cité Internationale de la Dentelle et de la Mode*, a museum that opened in 2010. The lace shown here is from Nancy Corzine. Hardware is by Houlès.

employ hundreds of artisans creating all manner of finery. Feathered trains for Oscar gowns, intricate organza camellias for chic suits, and python platforms studded with

a medley of rhinestones and metallic beads all fall within their exquisite realm.

In 2009, the Louis Vuitton *atelier* in Asnières marked its 150th anniversary. Dozens of craftspeople toil in the multilevel workshop, fashioning luxe bespoke pieces for clients all over the world. Celebrated creations include a monogrammed backpack for legendary photographer Annie Leibovitz and a carrying case designed for the precise measurements of a pair of bull terriers belonging to artistic director Marc Jacobs.

The splendid Asnières compound likewise houses a museum. Among the many treasures on exhibit is the historic Steamer bag that dates to 1901. In the workshop, meanwhile, towering windows look out onto manicured gardens where luggage makers cut the poplar used to make the frames of the Louis Vuitton iconic trunk. Like so many French *ateliers* past and present, it is a place where art meets commerce, where passionate artisanship and superlative design intersect.

Ambitious construction drawings act as the foundation for "Brasserie," white porcelain dinnerware from Pillivuyt. What is the difference between a brasserie, café and bistro? Well, brasseries are the city's original beer halls, not at all fancy, although nowadays they do dish up simple fare throughout the day. From there it gets more complicated, as both cafés and bistros also serve food and alcohol and are relatively affordable neighborhood spots. Cafés tend to serve sandwiches, pastries and perhaps a *plat du jour*. Think of popular, beyond chic Les Deux Magots and Café de Flore—where the literary and intellectual elite once rendezvoused. Both are cafés. In contrast, bistros have a more complete menu, generally are family owned and feature family recipes served family style, even to those dining alone. Almost certainly, the word *bistro* is rooted in *bistrouille*, French slang for a mixture of inexpensive brandy and coffee. So, then, it is probably correct to assume that many Parisians prefer dining at a café.

Aspiring to a life filled with beauty, we take Coco Chanel at her word: "There is no time for cut-and-dried monotony," she said. "There is time for work. And time for love. That leaves no other time." Roman shades—artfully embellished by Gillian Bradshaw Smith—drip in Décor de Paris's dazzling Swarovski crystals, catching the light and adding a touch of glamour. Swarovski's secret equation for transforming light is sheltered safely in the Austrian village of Wattens, wedged in the Alps.

Shapely, acrylic chairs from Allan Knight, Dallas, nip at waists and comfortably follow the contour of backs, making a strong fashion statement. To insure the chairs look their best from all angles, Houston artist Allan Rodewald added a soupçon of unexpected dash.

LEFT: Like most offices, this one includes the basics: computers, telephones and all-in-one printer, scanner, fax and copier. Surge protectors help avoid damage. Yet an office that is *all* business does not feel like a workplace—not when it is a playground for ideas. Desk lamps purchased in Paris are both functional and stylish. The *présentoir contemporain*, or contemporary display stand, from Michael Shannon & Associates, San Francisco, holds design-related materials.

A once unattractive cabinet is now unrecognizable, thanks to Sanders Studio, Dallas. Priming, painting, stenciling and glazing with old-world expertise clearly elevated its character.

FACING: A dazzling plaid is not the expected bathroom floor, but Waterworks offers plentiful proof that even the smallest bathroom can weave together a bit of uptown glam and a sophisticated look.

Hand-embroidered guest towels purchased in Paris depict two well-known landmarks: the Eiffel Tower and the basilica of Sacré-Coeur. The latter, a Roman Catholic church built from 1875–1914, stands in Montmartre, on a perilously steep street at the highest point of the French capital. Reportedly, an astonishing 10.5 million people visited in 2008. In comparison, 7 million visited the Eiffel Tower. Only Notre Dame had more sightseers, 13.6 million.

RIGHT: The basilica of Sacré-Coeur.

FACING: In eighteenth-century France, powder rooms were intended strictly for powdering one's wig. Nowadays the once-humble powder room invites admiration with Sherle Wagner gold-plated fixtures adorning a hand-carved brown onyx pedestal sink. The alabaster sconces are by Urban Archaeology and mirror is from ELG London, Ltd. Aviron's python scales the walls. Sheer window fabric (unseen) is by Rodolph.

A French state of mind brings a dash of hôtel glamour. Pool towels are by Louis Vuitton. Literary classics lie beneath cloth covers. Thanks to Sanders Studio, Dallas, a once unattractive cupboard morphed into a cabinet significantly more sophisticated. Ammonites (second shelf) are an extinct group of marine animals that are superb index fossils, linking the rock layer in which they are found to specific geological times. Their closest living relatives are the octopus, squid and cuttlefish.

EN PLEIN AIR

Water lilies, poppies, and tulips blossomed from the brushes of Claude Monet. Meadows of wild grasses, lavender fields and olive groves meanwhile fueled Pierre-Auguste Renoir's artistic passions. The most venerable French Impressionists of the nineteenth century, including Édouard Manet, Camille Pissarro and Paul Cézanne, reveled in nature's color and light. Though deemed unfashionable at the time, all opted to transport their canvases and easels, oils, palettes and talents outside—sketching and painting *en plein air*, ultimately capturing the environment's mysterious, ever-changing light and creating masterworks of the Impressionist movement.

A small flip-flop tray holds a poolside lunch, putting a relaxed spin on the expression "dining out." Striped fabric is from Clarence House.

FACING: Going green at the pool calls for Giati Designs' nine-foot-diameter Santa Barbara market umbrellas that offer protection from the sun, Perennials' fabrics that weather the season's spills and Murray's Iron Works furniture—table, chairs and chaises— every bit as comfortable as an indoor seating. Dry-fast cushions insure water flows quickly through mold-resistant channeled casing, thus the seating's down-like appearance.

Rebelling against the art establishment—the esteemed Paris *Salon*, where artists selected by a jury jostled for recognition—the Impressionists looked anew at France's charming villages, flourishing gardens and early bridges, as well as at the country's railway stations, cathedrals and cafés. While Paris was the epicenter of their avant-garde ambitions, rural communities along the River Seine—including Normandy and Versailles, a scant 16 kilometers (10 miles) outside Paris—quite naturally beckoned. >200

If this is not the year to fly into Roissy Charles de Gaulle Airport, rent an *appartement* and spend days taking cooking classes or language lessons, then from all appearances life can be blissful at home. Fondness for tanning was born when Coco Chanel returned from vacation on the French Riviera sheathed in an impossible-to-miss shade of brown; but, of course, we now know that sun worshipping is not in one's self-interest. Pool towels are from Louis Vuitton.

FACING: Crushed gravel chips line paths that wind their way to the pool and pool house.

Entertaining spills from the main house into a pool house, where the sound of music mingles with the soothing sound of water flowing from flush-mounted stream jets. Aruba Blue glass tile from Jeffrey Court blends with the pool's Mediterranean blue bottom. On deck is 12-inch by 24-inch Leuders limestone, quarried in Texas and laid in a herringbone pattern with Calico limestone trim and cabochons (oval, convex gems; smooth and not cut into facets). Since Leuders is denser than most other limestones, it absorbs less water and therefore maintains its natural appearance longer than many other natural stones. The nineteenth-century fountain is from Houston's Château Domingue, where 15,000 square feet of reclaimed building materials reside—all imported from France and other parts of Europe.

Decidedly French is an imposing Renaissance *château* that holds sway amid sculpted gardens in the heart of Dallas. To rise to the occasion in 2009, it borrowed understated elegance from the exterior of Chambord, the impressive Loire Valley castle built originally as a hunting lodge for Francis I, crowned king in 1515. Boosting *la maison*'s cachet is Savigny Rubamé limestone imported from France.

Much like the Impressionists seeking inspiration, each year an estimated three million admirers—some from within France but even more from outside it—wander through the Château de Versailles and then traverse its celebrated, meticulously planned grounds stretching across 1,700 acres. Regardless that the seven-hundred-room *château* and its grounds are now undergoing a $450 million make-over expected to take two decades, serious gardeners and aspiring artists gaze approvingly at the sculptures and fountains set in the impressive land, photographing in the changing light with hopes of improving their own environments or finding new ways to express their creativity. For the wonder and the dignity of Versailles makes that which is challenging seem attainable a continent away.

From Savannah to San Francisco and San Antonio in between, the classical influence of Versailles is easy to spot as residents adhere to the same key principles: logic, order, discipline and beauty. Whether land is rolling or flat, pea gravel paths separate well-defined patterns of squares and rectangles. Plantings sectioned geometrically into smaller beds captivatingly boast exacting mirror images. Statuary of mythological figures, graceful fountains and shapely urns spilling over with foliage lend dimension to sculptured, manicured estates surely less formal than the Palace of Versailles.

As if turning over a new leaf, Clarence House foliage weaves its way across a Murray's Iron Works sofa that rests on a Stark outdoor rug—it resists fading and mildew. In cooler months, a nineteenth-century limestone fireplace warms the open-air pavilion. Firescreen is from Murray's Iron Works.

In a testament to the park's varied beauty—carefully designed by the great landscape artist André Le Nôtre (1613–1700) more than three hundred years ago—savvy Americans borrow the principles he preached, published in *La Theorie et La Pratique du Jardinage* in 1739 by one of his pupils.

As it is, Le Nôtre's artistic guidelines are as practical today as when they held sway in the seventeenth century. In short, he believed that aesthetic rewards come from a garden in harmony with the setting; planned with the climate in mind; in scale with the house; and, not least, fitting the needs and lifestyle of the owner, which was his way of saying in keeping with an ability to care properly for the land.

In creating his masterpieces, Le Nôtre laid the foundation for classical French gardens based on his conviction that man had the ability to dominate nature. Repeatedly employing the same standard plan, a *château* served as the design's central focus, with a central axis leading toward the structure, bisected by diverging paths. Each terrace, whether ascending or descending, helped create the optical illusion of infinite space without diminishing the size of the main house.

Moving one's attention for detail outside results in an outdoor room that looks equally suited for indoors. Wooden wine corks from South of Market, Atlanta, rest in a round rush basket from Mecox Gardens, Dallas. Vases are from Bergdorf Goodman, NYC. Old tree slices were found on opposite coasts—first at Martin Showroom in Saint Helena, California, then later at Holly Hunt in New York City.

Born in Paris into a family of royal gardeners, André Le Nôtre was an obvious choice to succeed his father, Jean Le Nôtre, at the Jardin des Tuileries when the latter became chief gardener to Louis XIII. In like manner, Jean Le Nôtre had quite naturally assumed his own father's role at Tuileries Gardens, when summoned in 1592 to serve as landscaper to Queen Marie de Médici (1575–1642), Henri IV's second wife and Louis XIV's grandmother.

No, this is not the French Riviera's latest escape. Nor is authentic French fare available at this waterside café. But one can have lunch alfresco sans the strict formality often linked to the French in a setting that is *très* French, *très chic*, thanks to Houston artist Allan Rodewald.

A gifted engineer with an artist's eye, André Le Nôtre set about in 1637 revamping the Tuileries—originally the city's 63-acre garbage dump with clay soil used for making *tuiles* (tiles); hence its name. Before long, the regal avenue des Champs-Élysées would also bear his hallmark, as he gave the broad boulevard even more presence by lacing it with parallel rows of chestnut trees and planting generous sweeps of brilliant-colored flowers. >211

FACING: Making an apt splash at a table that sits just a few yards from the pool is an array of entrées, salads and desserts that give a solid fabric an edge.

In collaboration with nature, a pool house open to the elements is more than an imposing accessory to the house. With a fully equipped summer kitchen and an array of notable amenities, including a flat-screen television and comfortable, stylish seating, it is perfect for casual entertaining. The clock once hung in a train station in France.

Scalamandré's frogs have fun in the sun, hopping unapologetically onto bar stools within easy reach of bumblebee petit fours from Dallas Affaires Cake Company.

A child-friendly changing room keeps clothes from being tossed onto the floor or into any old locker —handpainted by Gillian Bradshaw Smith. "Scuba" wallcovering is from Brentano.

FACING: Today's tile choices go beyond traditional glazed ceramics with an array of new options gaining popularity. To be sure, "Pebble Tile" displays more oomph than average. But, then, so do the pedestal sink, mirror, shelf and grooming bar, all in polished nickel, the fashionable finish, and all from Waterworks. Flip-flop soap for this pool bath is from Bestbeachweddingfavors.com.

Doors that once might have revealed gleaming black carriages now open to a parking garage. Handcrafted ring pulls are from Rocky Mountain Hardware.

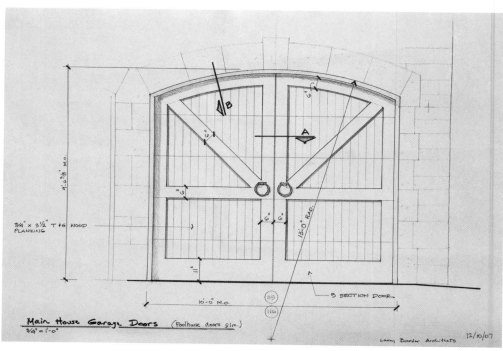

Main House Garage Doors (Poolhouse doors sim.)
3/4" = 1'-0"

Larry Boerder Architects   12/10/07

In the meantime, he worked feverishly from 1656 to 1661 producing an extraordinary masterpiece for Nicholas Fouquet (1615–80), who served as minister of finance under Louis XIV. At Vaux-le-Vicomte, in Seine-et-Marne south of Paris, Le Nôtre redirected one of two rivers traversing the unspoiled terrain. Also, he carefully arranged a hierarchy of small spaces spawned from a central axis sweeping away from the grand *château* as far as the eye could see. Flower-banked reflecting pools, basins and waterfalls, plus 1,200 fountains offered further proof of his imaginative hand.

Considering that everyone knew subjects were not to live more lavishly than the king, it may not have come as surprising news that Louis XIV sent for the artist responsible for the landscaping at Vaux-le-Vicomte and instructed him to exceed all prior triumphs at Versailles, where much of the land was a swamp. And indeed he did. Over the next thirty-three years, Le Nôtre's laborers and he gradually installed elaborate French gardens, laying out spacious terraces and *parterres* with winding pebble paths and coppices, while turning marshes into imposing ornamental lakes, beautified with fountains and sculptures. Never mind that the decorative lakes necessitated funneling water via an aqueduct and network of pipes from the town of Marly (now Marly-le-Roi), roughly six kilometers away.

Tree-lined forests, fruit groves and impressive stone stairways traded on the king's desire for over-the-top extravagance, consciously or not. There were stately shrubs, sumptuous flowerbeds and topiaries fashioned into sculpted shapes. Musical water fountains sprung to life, dancing in the air when the king approached; 460 of them are still working today. But perhaps most notably, Le Nôtre created a predilection for French gardens when most of the world was still enamored with Italian ones.

When André Le Nôtre died in 1700, France mourned the loss of the famous seventeenth-century landscape architect. Yet his unprecedented influence has not faded with time, as people from around the world and from all occupations continue taking their cues from his awe-inspiring designs at the sprawling Palace of Versailles.

Needlepoint ivy and purple asters spill from a classically inspired stone urn with automatic irrigation. Drain lines stubbed from the column below connect through the base of the planter, providing a clean supply and exit for water.

Sumptuous guest room accommodations offer a view of a *parterre* masterfully planned by Harold Leidner Company, landscape architects.

LEFT: A driveway takes its cue from one of Paris's nearly 6,000 cobbled streets, where four- to five-inch granite *pavé mosaïque* (cubes), are laid in a pattern resembling a peacock's tail. The tumbled Ozark cobblestones shown here are 6 x 6 inches.

Vocabulaire du Jardinage

Here are just a few of the many garden tools commonly used to enhance spaces *en plein air*.

ALLÉE: A tree-lined walk, avenue or wide path that brings grandeur to an entrance or frames a garden.

ARBOR: (*Tonnelle* in French.) An outdoor room framed in latticework from which bougainvillea, wisteria or other entwined climbing vines cascade, shading the setting.

BOSQUET: A carefully planned ornamental grove of trees—generally a single variety—pruned and planted in a formal grid and pierced by paths, thus creating an open-air drawing room. At Versailles, sculptures and fountains stand among the trees.

BOWER: A shelter akin to an arbor but shaped from entwined tree boughs or vines rather than supported by latticework.

BOXWOODS: Various species of evergreen shrubs favored for hedges and topiaries in formal gardens, generally planted in orderly grids, then clipped and coaxed into geometric shapes such as domes or globes.

BRODERIE: French for "embroidery." Formal, embellished *parterres* (flower beds) bordered by tidy clipped hedges or pruned shrubs and pebble paths, forming an elaborate ornamental motif suggestive of embroidery.

CALADES: River pebbles set into mortar in curving patterns, forming paths and terraces, particularly in Provence.

CALPINAGE: Bricks laid on edge, often in a herringbone pattern—commonly seen on paths and terraces in Provence.

CLÔTURE VIVANTE: French for "living fence," commonly created by weaving shrub branches together.

COURTYARD: A cobblestone area behind imposing, heavily carved *hôtel particulier* doors, where carriages stood waiting in the nineteenth century. Today, however, the building most likely houses separate living areas, while pale gravel or cobblestones offer a parking spot for cars in an open space surrounded by walls.

ESPALIER: From the Latin *spatula,* meaning shoulder blade. Thus, plantings—most often fruit trees but shrubs too—trained to grow flat against a support.

EVERGREENS: Shrubs favored for hedges and topiaries. Evergreens are one of the most distinctive features of classical French gardens, since they can be enjoyed year-round.

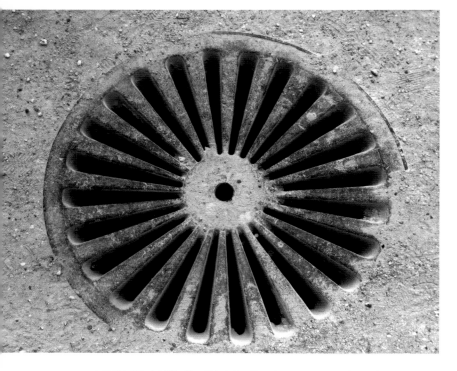

ABOVE AND FACING: Perhaps predictably, considering the grandeur of Paris, visually appealing drains crafted with an eye for presence sit amongst the topiary sculptures that watch over the perfectly groomed boxwoods in the *Jardin des Tuileries.* Stretching from the Louvre to the Place de la Concorde, the garden graces 25 hectares (or about 63 acres), and to this day closely follows the design laid out in 1637 by landscape artist André Le Nôtre (1613–1700).

FLOWERS: Until the 19th century, flowerbeds were not the focus of gardens. In fact, Louis XIV disliked flowers.

GAZEBO: A freestanding, fanciful house open on all sides, often sited at the corner of a garden, where it frequently stands sometimes two stories tall.

GROTTE (feminine, grotto): A cave-like structure designed to provide a cool respite during warm weather.

HEDGE: A dense row of shrubs that frames plantings or establishes the limits of a garden, much like a wall. Low hedges, such as boxwood, often section interior areas of a garden. Considered most formal are sheared yew, privet and beech hedges.

JARDINIÈRE: An ornamental stand or container for flowers or plants, generally porcelain, that became popular in late-eighteenth-century France.

LE JARDIN D'HERBES: Herb garden.

LOGGIA: An open-sided shelter either freestanding or siding a house, suitable for use as an outdoor sitting room as well as for entertaining. A roof protects against the rain.

PARTERRE: French for "on the ground." A level garden bed—typically made up of flowers—with winding pebble paths geometrically dividing the plan. Seventeenth-century baroque textile patterns and hand-forged ironwork designs often copied the ornate, swirling patterns of *parterres* in France.

PATH: A pebble walkway that divides planting beds and draws the eye to the farthest reaches.

PATTE D'OIE: The place where three, four or five straight allées, or avenues, meet at sharp angles and form a shape similar to a goose's foot.

PERGOLA: An open-roofed structure fashioned with beams and cross members supported by a row of pillars or posts, from which flowers or plants cascade, creating a covered walkway.

POTAGER: A kitchen garden that provides vegetables and herbs for mealtime consumption. Rooted in Italian gardens cultivated by monks and nuns, *potagers* supplied inhabitants of the abbeys with food and altars with flowers. At Versailles stands a statue of Jean-Baptiste de la Quintinie, Louis XIV's chief gardener and the creator of his ornamental kitchen garden.

STATUARY: Likenesses of liberators and public symbols, as well as mythological figures and animals, important to French heritage.

TOPIARY: Trees and shrubbery fashioned into ornamental sculpted shapes. Sometimes set in large planters.

TREILLAGE: Elaborate trelliswork, either freestanding or placed against a fence or wall, often designed to create depth and perspective.

TRELLIS: Any two-dimensional frame of latticework, whether freestanding or attached to a wall or fence.

URNS: A vessel varying in size and shape, usually on a footed base or pedestal.

Resources

When it comes to shopping, here are some of the many stateside places where we go in search of accessories, antiques, bath fittings, fabrics, furniture, linens, trimmings and more—always with furniture plans in hand, specifying sizes. And here are the artisans we rely on. In addition, we log frequent-flier miles traveling abroad.

ANTIQUE FURNISHINGS AND ACCESSORIES

Agostino Antiques, Ltd.
21 Broad St.
Red Bank, NJ 07701
Telephone 732.345.7301
agostinoantiques.com

Ambiance Antiques
550 15th St. #1
San Francisco, CA 94103
Telephone 415.626.0145
ambianceantiques.com

Anthony Antiques & Fine Arts
401 E. 200 S.
Salt Lake City, UT 84111
Telephone 801.328.2231
anthonysfineart.com

Area
5600 Kirby Dr.
Houston, TX 77005
Telephone 713.668.1668

Bremermann Designs
3943 Magazine St.
New Orleans, LA 70115
Telephone 504.891.7763
bremermanndesigns.com

Brian Stringer Antiques
2031 W. Alabama St.
Houston, TX 77006
Telephone 713.526.7380
brianstringersantiques.com

Carl Moore Antiques
1610 Bissonnet St.
Houston, TX 77005
Telephone 713.524.2502
carlmooreantiques.com

Charles Gaylord & Co.
Two Henry Adams St., Ste. 406
San Francisco, CA 94103
Telephone 415.861.6300
charlesgaylord.com

Château Domingue
3615-B W. Alabama St.
Houston, TX 77027
Telephone 713.961.3444
chateaudomingue.com

Country French Interiors
1428 Slocum St.
Dallas, TX 75207
Telephone 214.747.4700
countryfrenchinteriors.com

Décor de France
24 N. Blvd. of the Presidents
Sarasota, FL 34236
Telephone 941.388.1599
decordefrance.com

DHS Designs, Inc.
6521 Friel Rd.
Queenstown, MD 21658
Telephone 410.827.8167
dhsdesigns.com

Donald J. Embree Antiques
1115 Slocum St.
Dallas, TX 75207
Telephone 214.760.9141

Duane Antiques
176 Duane St.
New York, NY 10013
Telephone 212.625.8066
duaneantiques.com

East & Orient Company
1123 Slocum St.
Dallas, TX 75207
Telephone 214.741.1191
eastandorient.com

Ed Hardy San Francisco
188 Henry Adams St.
San Francisco, CA 94103
Telephone 415.626.6300
edhardysf.com

Erin Martin Showroom
1350 Main St.
St. Helena, CA 94574
Telephone 707.967.8782
martinshowroom.com

The Gables
711 Miami Cr.
Atlanta, GA 30324
Telephone 800.753.3342
thegablesantiques.com

Galerie Maurmo
301 South County Rd.
Palm Beach, FL 33480
Telephone 561.202.6122

Gore Dean Antiques
2828 Pennsylvania Ave.
Washington, DC 20007
Telephone 202.625.9199
goredeanantiques.com

The Gray Door
3465-A W. Alabama St.
Houston, TX 77019
Telephone 713.521.9085
graydoorantiques.com

Inessa Stewart Antiques
5330 Bluebonnet Blvd.
Baton Rouge, LA 70809
Telephone 225.368.8600

5201 W. Lovers Ln.
Dallas, TX 75209
Telephone 214.366.2660
inessa.com

Jacqueline Adams Antiques
The Galleries of Peachtree Hills
425 Peachtree Hills Ave.
Atlanta, GA 30305
Telephone 404.869.6790
jacquelineadamsantiques.com

Jane Moore Interiors
2922 Virginia St.
Houston, TX 77098
Telephone 713.526.6113

Jefferson West Inc.
9310 Jefferson Blvd.
Culver City, CA 90232
Telephone 310.558.3031
jeffersonwest.com

John Rosselli & Associates
306 East 61st St., Ground Fl.
New York, NY 10065
Telephone 212.750.0060

979 3rd Ave.,18th Fl.
New York, NY 10022
Telephone 212.593.2060
johnrosselliantiques.com

Joseph Minton Antiques
1410 Slocum St.
Dallas, TX 75207
Telephone 214.744.3111
mintonantiques.com

Joyce Horn Antiques
1022 Wirt Rd., Ste. 326
Houston, TX 77055
Telephone 713.688.0507
joycehornantiques.com

Color-saturated Pantone coffee mugs and bursts of paint chips team with Limoges dinnerware for Bergdorf Goodman. For the artist's table, "Sandrine Ganem" Paris with *les couleurs* of France— *vert, bleu, jaune* and more—radiates a painterly look.

Kay O'Toole Antiques
1921 Westheimer Rd.
Houston, TX 77098
Telephone 713.523.1921
kayotooleantiques.com

Kendall Wilkinson Home
3419 Sacramento St.
San Francisco, CA 94118
Telephone 415.409.2299
kendallwilkinson.com

Le Louvre French Antiques
1400 Slocum St.
Dallas, TX 75207
Telephone 214.742.2605
lelouvre-antiques.com

Legacy Antiques
1406 Slocum St.
Dallas, TX 75207
Telephone 214.748.4606
legacyantiques.com

The Lotus Collection
445 Jackson St.
San Francisco, CA 94111
Telephone 415.398.8115
ktaylor-lotus.com

Lovers Lane Antique Market
5001 W. Lovers Ln.
Dallas, TX 75209
Telephone 214.351.5656
loverslaneantiques.com

M. Naeve Antiques
1926 Bissonnet St.
Houston, TX 77005
Telephone 713.524.0990

Maison Felice
73-960 El Paseo
Palm Desert, CA 92260
Telephone 760.862.0021
maisonfelice.com

Mariette Himes Gomez
506 E. 74th St.
New York, NY 10021
Telephone 212.288.6856
gomezassociates.com

Marston Luce
1651 Wisconsin Ave., N.W.
Washington, DC 20007
Telephone 202.333.6800
marstonluce.com

The McNally Company Antiques
6033 L&M Paseo Delicias
Rancho Santa Fe, CA 92067
Telephone 858.756.1922
mcnallycompanyantiques.com

Metropolitan Artifacts, Inc.
Architectural Antiques
4783 Peachtree Rd.
Atlanta, GA 30341
Telephone 770.986.0007
metropolitanartifacts.com

The Mews
1708 Market Center Blvd.
Dallas, TX 75207
Telephone 214.748.9070
themews.net

Neal & Co.
4502 Greenbriar St.
Houston, TX 77005
Telephone 713.942.9800

Newell Art Galleries, Inc.
425 E. 53rd St.
New York, NY 10022
Telephone 212.758.1970
newel.com

Niall Smith
306 E. 61st St.
New York, NY 10021
Telephone 212.750.3985

Nick Brock Antiques
2909 N. Henderson St.
Dallas, TX 75206
Telephone 214.828.0624
nickbrockantiquesonline.com

Parc Monceau, Ltd.
425 Peachtree Hills Ave., # 15
Atlanta, GA 30305
Telephone 404.467.8107
parcmonceauatl.com

Parkhouse Antiques
114 Parkhouse St.
Dallas, TX 75207
Telephone 214.741.1199
parkhouseantiques.com

Mercato Italian Antiques & Artifacts
33071 W. 83rd St.
De Soto, KS 66018
Telephone 913.583.1511
mercatoantiques.com

Petricia Thompson Antiques
3522 Magazine St.
New Orleans, LA 70115
Telephone 504.897.5477
petriciathompsonantiques.com

Pied-A-Terre
7645 Girard Ave.
La Jolla, CA 92037
Telephone 858.456.4433

Pittet & Co.
1215 Slocum St.
Dallas, TX 75207
Telephone 214.748.8999
pittet.com

R.F. Imports
5950 Berkshire Ln., Ste. 1500
Dallas, TX 75225
Telephone 214.696.0152

Ronnie and Guy Weil Antiques
PO Box 583
Newhope, PA 18938
Telephone 215.862.9421
ronnieandguyweilantiq
ues.1stdibs.com

Skelton St. John
2143 Westheimer Rd.
Houston, TX 77098
Telephone 713.524.1990

South of Market
345 Peachtree Hills Ave.
Atlanta, GA 30305
Telephone 404.995.9399
southofmarket.biz

The Stalls
116 Bennett St.
Atlanta, GA 30309
Telephone 404.352.4430
thestalls.com

Studio Veneto
7427 Girard Ave.
La Jolla, CA 92037
858.551.2782
studioveneto.com

Tara Shaw Antiques
1845-A W. Alabama St.
Houston, TX 77098
Telephone 713.533.9744
tarashaw.com

Therien & Co.
716. N. La Cienega Blvd.
Los Angeles, CA 90069
Telephone 310.657.4615

411 Vermont St.
San Francisco, CA 94103
Telephone 415.956.8850
therien.com

Tres Belle
2435 East Coast Hwy.
Corona Del Mar, CA 92625
Telephone 949.723.0022
tresbelleantiques.com

Uncommon Market, Inc.
2701-2707 Fairmount St.
Dallas, TX 75201
Telephone 214.871.2775
uncommonmarketinc.com

W. Gardner, Ltd.
2930 Ferndale Pl.
Houston, TX 77098
Telephone 713.521.1027
wgardnerltd.com

Watkins Culver
2308 Bissonnet St.
Houston, TX 77005
Telephone 713.529.0597
watkinsculver.com

The Whimsey Shoppe Slocum
1444 Oak Lawn Ave.
Dallas, TX 75207
Telephone 214.745.1800
thewhimseyshoppe.com

ARTISANS

Allan Rodewald
Expressive Design Studios
1402 Dart St.
Houston, TX 77007
Telephone 713.501.6613
Allanrodewald.com

Authentic Joinery & Millwork, LLC.
1266 West Paces Ferry Rd. #563
Atlanta, GA 30327
Telephone 404.841.4818
ajm-llc.com

Brad Oldham, Inc.
2603 Farrington St.
Dallas, TX 75207
Telephone 214.239.3993
bradoldham.com

Chuck Walter
511 S. Elm St.
Arlington, TX 76010
Telephone 817.229.9453

Daniel Heath
4624 Charles Pl.
Plano, TX 75093
Telephone 214.697.4489
heathwatercolors.com

David Lyles
514 Summit Dr.
Richardson, TX 75081
Telephone 972.841.0463
seedavidlyles.com

Ebenisterie Bertoli
Route de Valliguieres
Tavel, France 30126
Telephone 33.4.66.50.03.42

Gillian Bradshaw Smith
311 N. Winnetka Ave.
Dallas, TX 75208
Telephone 214.948.8472
gillianbradshaw-smith.net

Irene de Watteville
749 N. Granados Ave.
Solana Beach, CA 92075
Telephone 858.755.0627

Jackie Musso
6530 St. Moritz Ave.
Dallas, TX 75214
Telephone 214.828.1249

Jennifer Chapman Designs
7049 Via Cabana
Carlsbad, CA 92009
Telephone 760.602.0079
jenniferchapmandesign.com

Jo Mattison
4100 San Carlos St.
Dallas, TX 75205
Telephone 214.354.3527
jomattisonart.com

Joanna Otte Studios
3820 Ridgehaven Rd.
Fort Worth, TX 76116
Telephone 817.235.8233

Kay Fox's Custom Creations
2404 Springpark Way
Richardson, TX 75082
Telephone 972.437.4227

Patrick Edwards
3815 Utah St.
San Diego, CA 92104
Telephone 619.298.0864
wpatrickedwards.com

Paul J. Labadie
1315 Conant St.
Dallas, TX 75207
Telephone 214.905.9455

Sanders Studio
PO Box 670501
Dallas, TX 75367
Telephone: 972.233.1777
sanders-studio.com

Shaun Christopher Designs
6593 Garlinghouse Ln.
Dallas, TX 75252
Telephone 214.597.9059
shaun-christopher.com

Straight Stitch
2910 Belmeade Dr., Ste. 105
Carrollton, TX 75006
Telephone 972.416.6124

BATH FITTINGS

Czech & Speake
1 Design Center Pl., Ste. 429
Boston, MA 02210
Telephone 800.632.4165
czechandspeake.com

Herbeau Creations of America
3600 Westview Dr.
Naples, FL 34104
Telephone 800.547.1608
herbeau.com

Kallista, Inc.
1227 North 8th St., Ste. 2
Sheboygan, WI 53081
Telephone 888.4.Kallista
kallistainc.com

Sherle Wagner, International
300 E. 62nd St.
New York, NY 10065
Telephone 212.758.3300
sherlewagner.com

Sunrise Specialty
930 98th Ave.
Oakland, CA 94603
Telephone 510.729.7277
sunrisespecialty.com

Urban Archeology
143 Franklin St.
New York, NY 10013
Telephone 212.431.4646
urbanarcheology.com

Waterworks
60 Backus Ave.
Danbury, CT 06810
Telephone 800.899.6757
waterworks.com

CARPETS

Abrash Rugs
1025 N. Stemmons Frwy., Ste. 760
Dallas, TX 75207
Telephone 214.573.6262
abrashrugs.com

Asmara, Inc.
88 Black Falcon Ave.
Boston, MA 02210
Telephone 800.451.7240
asmarainc.com

Beauvais Carpets
The Fuller Building
595 Madison Ave., 3rd Fl.
New York, NY 10022
Telephone 212.688.2265
beauvaiscarpets.com

Carol Piper Rugs, Inc.
1809 W. Gray St.
Houston, TX 77019
Telephone 713.524.2442
carolpiperrugs.com

Design Materials
241 S. 55th St.
Kansas City, KA 66106
Telephone 913.342.9796
dmifloors.com

Farzin Rugs & Design
1414 Slocum St.
Dallas, TX 75207
Telephone 214.747.1511

Hokanson
Decorative Ctr.
5120 Woodway Rd. #190
Houston, TX 77056
Telephone 800.255.5720
hokansoncarpet.com

Mansour
8600 Melrose Ave.
Los Angeles, CA 90069
Telephone 310.652.9999
mansourrug.com

Mark, Inc.
34 E. Putnam Ave.
Greenwich, CT 06830
Telephone 203.861.0110
markinccarpets.com

Matt Camron Rugs and Tapestries
2702 Sackett St.
Houston, TX 77098
mattcamron.com

Nouri & Sons Antique Oriental Rugs
3001 Richmond
Houston, TX 77098
Telephone 713.523.6626
nouriantiquerugs.com

Renaissance Collection
1532 Hi Line Dr.
Dallas, TX 75207
Telephone 214.698.1000
rencollection.com

Rosecore Carpet Co., Inc.
79 Madison Ave., 15th Fl.
New York, NY 10016
Telephone 800.523.1200
rosecore.com

Stark Carpet
D&D Building
979 Third Ave.
New York, NY 10022
Telephone 212.752.9000
starkcarpet.com

Stephen Miller Gallery
800 Santa Cruz Ave.
Menlo Park, CA 94025
Telephone 650.327.5040
stephenmillergallery.com

DECORATIVE HARDWARE

E. R. Butler & Co., Inc.
38 Charles St.
Boston, MA 02114
Telephone 617.722.0230
erbutler.com

Manor House
188 S. Main St.
Collierville, TN 38017
Telephone 901.861.1957
manorhouseusa.com

Nanz Custom Hardware
20 Vandam St.
New York, NY 10013
Telephone 212.367.7000
nanz.com

P. E. Guerin, Inc.
21-23 Jane St.
New York, NY 10014
Telephone 212.243.5270
peguerin.com

Palmer Designs
7863 Herschel Ave.
La Jolla, CA 92037
Telephone 858.551.1350
palmer-design.com

Pierce Hardware
6823 Snider Plaza
Dallas, TX 75205
Telephone 214.368.2851
piercehardware.com

FABRICS & FURNITURE

Anna French
36 Hinton Rd.
London, SE24 0HJ
Telephone 020.7737.6555
annafrench.co.uk

Allan Knight & Associates
150 Turtle Creek Blvd., Ste. 101
Dallas, Texas 75207
Telephone 214.741.2227
allanknightasso.com

B. Berger Fabrics
1380 Highland Rd.
Macedonia, OH 44056
Telephone 330.425.3838
bberger.com

Beacon Hill
225 Foxboro Blvd.
Foxboro, MA 02035
Telephone 800.333.3777
beaconhilldesign.com

Bennison Fabrics, Inc.
232 E. 59th St.
New York, NY 10022
Telephone 212.223.0373
bennisonfabrics.com

Antique gold Louis XVI crémone bolts from P. E. Guerin bring a touch of drama to the serene decor. The Library of Congress recommends maintaining a book room at 60 to 70 degrees Fahrenheit with 65 percent relative humidity—as dry heat will cause pages to become brittle, while moist heat prompts mold and insects. Equally important, books will fade in direct light.

Bergamo Fabrics, Inc.
265 Washington St.
Mount Vernon, NY 10553
Telephone 914.665.0800
bergamofabrics.com

Boussac Fadini
1692 Chantilly Dr. #C
Atlanta, GA 30324
Telephone 866.707.1524
pierrefrey.com

Brentano Inc.
260 Holbrook Dr.
Wheeling, IL 60090
Telephone 847.657.8481
brentanofabrics.com

Brunschwig & Fils, Inc.
75 Virginia Rd.
North White Plains, NY 10603
Telephone 914.684.5800
brunschwig.com

The Budji Collections, Inc.
7302 E. Helm Dr., Ste. 2002
Scottsdale, AZ 85260-3126
Telephone 480.905.3126
budji.com

The Cameron Collection
150 Dallas Design Center
1025 N. Stemmons Frwy.
Dallas, TX 75207
Telephone 214.744.1544
cameroncollection.com

Carlton V, Ltd.
D&D Building
979 Third Ave., 15th Fl.
New York, NY 10022
Telephone 212.355.4525
carletonvltd.com

The French credit Catherine de Medici for introducing them to a delicate fabric with small holes between the threads and tiny teeth around the edges, which they promptly named *dentelle* and deemed worthy of being seen.

Charles Pollock
Reproductions, Inc.
6824 Lexington Ave.
Los Angeles, CA 90038
Telephone 323.962.0440
charlespollockrepro.com

Christopher Hyland, Inc.
D&D Building
979 Third Ave., Ste. 1710
New York, NY 10022
Telephone 212.688.6121
christopherhyland.com

Christopher Norman, Inc.
D&D Building
979 Third Ave., Ste. 1200
New York, NY 10022
Telephone 212.644.5301
christophernorman.com

Clarence House, Inc.
D&D Building
979 Third Ave., Ste. 205
New York, NY 10022
Telephone 212.752.2890
clarencehouse.com

Classic Revivals, Inc.
One Design Center Pl., Ste. 534
Boston, MA 02210
Telephone 617.574.9030
classicrevivals.com

Coraggio Textiles
PO Box 3332
Bellevue, WA 98009
Telephone 800.624.2420
coraggio.com

Cowtan & Tout
111 Eighth Ave., Ste. 930
New York, NY 10011
Telephone 212.647.6900
cowtan.com

Delany & Long, Ltd.
41 Chestnut St.
Greenwich, CT 06830
Telephone 203.532.0010
delanyandlong.com

Dennis & Leen
8734 Melrose Ave.
Los Angeles, CA 90069
Telephone 310.652.0855
dennisandleen.com

Donghia, Inc.
256 Washington St.
Mount Vernon, NY 10553
Telephone 914.662.2377
donghia.com

Elizabeth Dow, Ltd.
11 Indian Wells Hwy.
PO Box 2310
Amagansett, NY 11930
Telephone 631.267.3401
elizabethdow.com

Erika Brunson
5115 W. Adams Blvd.
Los Angeles, CA 90016
Telephone 323.931.3225
erikabrunson.com

F. Schumacher Company
79 Madison Ave., 14th Fl.
New York, NY 10016
Telephone 212.213.7900
fschumacher.com

The Farmhouse Collection, Inc.
PO Box 3089
Twin Falls, ID 83303
Telephone 208.736.8700
farmhousecollection.com

The Florio Collection
8815 Dorrington Ave.
West Hollywood, CA 90048
Telephone 310.273.8003
floriocollection.com

Fortuny, Inc.
D&D Building
979 Third Ave., 16th Fl.
New York, NY 10022
Telephone 212.753.7153
fortuny.com

Gregorius/ Pineo
653 N. La Cienega Blvd.
Los Angeles, CA 90069
Telephone 310.659.0588
gregoriuspineo.com

Hamilton, Inc.
8417 Melrose Pl.
Los Angeles, CA 90069
Telephone 323.655.9193
thehouseofhamilton.net

Henry Calvin Fabrics
2046 Lars Way
Medford, OR 97501
Telephone 541.732.1996
Telephone 888.732.1996 (toll-free)
henrycalvin.com

Hinson & Company
2735 Jackson Ave.
Long Island City, NY 11101
Telephone 718.482.1100
hinsonco.com

Holly Hunt
801 W. Adams
Chicago, IL 60607
Telephone 800.320.3145
hollyhunt.com

Indulge Maison Decor
2903 Saint St.
Houston, TX 77027
713.888.0181
indulgedecor.com

J. Robert Scott
500 N. Oak St.
Inglewood, CA 90302
Telephone 310.680.4300
jrobertscott.com

Jagtar
351 Peachtree Hills Ave. N.E.
Suite 125
Atlanta, GA 30305
Telephone 404.261.5116
jagtar.com

Jan Barboglio
145 Cole Ave.
Dallas, TX 75207
Telephone 214.698.1920

Jane Keltner
94 Cumberland Blvd.
Memphis, TN 38112
Telephone 800.487.8033
janekeltner.com

Jane Shelton
205 Catchings Ave.
Indianola, MS 38751
Telephone 800.530.7259
janeshelton.com

Jim Thompson
1694 Chantilly Dr.
Atlanta, GA 30324
Telephone 800.262.0336
jimthompson.com

John Derian
6 East 2nd St.
New York, NY 10003
Telephone 212.677.3917
johnderian.com

Kravet Fabrics, Inc.
225 Central Ave. S.
Bethpage, NY 11714
Telephone 516.293.2000
kravet.com

La Lune Collection
930 E. Burleigh St.
Milwaukee, WI 53212
Telephone 414.263.5300
lalunecollection.com

Lee Jofa
225 Central Ave. So.
Bethpage, NY 11714
Telephone 800.453.3563
leejofa.com

Lelievre
D&D Building
979 3rd Ave.,10th Fl.
New York, NY 10022
Telephone 212.355.7186
starkfabric.com

Malabar Fabrics
8A Trowbridge Dr.
Bethel, CT 06801
Telephone 877.625.2227
malabar.co.uk

Manuel Canovas
111 Eighth Ave., Ste. 930
New York, NY 10011
Telephone 212.647.6900
manuelcanovas.com

Marroquin Custom Upholstery
4835 Reading St.
Dallas, TX 75247
Telephone 214.905.0461
marroquincustomuph.com

Marvic Textiles, Ltd.
1 Westpoint Trading Estate
Alliance Rd.
Acton, London W3 ORA
UK
Telephone 44.20.8993.0191
marvictextiles.co.uk

Mecox
4532 Cole Ave.
Dallas, TX 75205
Telephone 214.580.3800
Mecoxgardens.com

Michael Shannon Associates
722 Steiner St.
San Francisco, CA 94117
Telephone 415.563.2727
s-j.com

Michael Taylor Designs
155 Rhode Island St.
San Francisco, CA 94103
Telephone 415.558.9940
michaeltaylordesigns.com

Minton Spidell, Inc.
8467 Steller Dr.
Culver City, CA 90232
Telephone 310.836.0403
minton-spidell.com

Mokum Textiles
98 Barcom Ave.
Rushcutters Bay NSW 2011
Telephone 866.523.4437
mokumtextiles.com

Murray's Iron Works
1801 E. 50th St.
Los Angeles, CA 90058
Telephone 323.521.1140
murraysiw.com

Nancy Corzine
256 W. Ivy Ave.
Inglewood, CA 90302
Telephone 310.672.6775
nancycorzine.com

Niermann Weeks
Fine Arts Building
232 E. 59th St.
New York, NY 10022
Telephone 212.319.7979
niermannweeks.com

Nobilis, Inc.
3006 Emrick Blvd.
Bethlehem, PA 18020
Telephone 800.464.6670
nobilis.fr

Old Timber Table Company
908 Dragon St.
Dallas, TX 75207
Telephone 214.761.1882
oldtimbertable.com

Old World Weavers
D&D Building
979 Third Ave., 10th Fl.
New York, NY 10022
Telephone 212.752.9000
old-world-weavers.com

Osborne & Little
90 Commerce Rd.
Stamford, CT 06902
Telephone 203.359.1500
osborneandlittle.com

Palecek
601 Parr Blvd.
Richmond, CA 94801
Telephone 800.274.7730
palecek.com

Patina, Inc.
351 Peachtree Hills Ave., N.E.
Atlanta, GA 30305
Telephone 404.261.5932
patinainc.com

Perennials Outdoor Fabrics
140 Regal Row
Dallas, TX 75247
Telephone 214.638.4162
perennialsfabrics.com

Peter Fasano, Ltd.
964 S. Main St.
Great Barrington, MA 01230
Telephone 413.528.6872
peterfasano.com

Pierre Frey, Ltd.
12 E. 32nd St.
New York, NY 10016
Telephone 212.213.3099
pierrefrey.com

Pindler & Pindler, Inc.
11910 Poindexter Ave.
Moorpark, CA 93021
Telephone 805.531.9090
pindler.com

Pizitz Home & Cottage
121 Central Square
Seaside, FL 32459
Telephone 850.231.2240

Pollack & Associates
150 Varick St.
New York, NY 10013
Telephone 212.627.7766
pollackassociates.com

Rose Tarlow Textiles
8540 Melrose Ave.
Los Angeles, CA 90069
Telephone 323.651.2202
rosetarlow.com

Scalamandré
350 Wireless Blvd.
Hauppauge, NY 11788
Telephone 631.467.8800
scalamandre.com

Scully & Scully
504 Park Ave.
New York, NY 10022
Telephone 800.223.3717
scullyandscully.com

Sea Cloth
201 Central Ave S.
Bethpage, NY 11714
Telephone 800.453.3563
seacloth.com

The Silk Trading Co.
360 S. La Brea Ave.
Los Angeles, CA 90036
Telephone 323.954.9280
silktrading.com

Smith & Watson
200 Lexington Ave., Ste. 801
New York, NY 10016
Telephone 212.686.6444
smith-watson.com

Stroheim & Romann, Inc.
30-30 47th Ave.
New York, NY 11101
Telephone 718.706.7000
stroheim.com

Summer Hill, Ltd
101 Henry Adams St. #272
San Francisco, CA 94103
Telephone 415.355.1300
summerhill.com

Travers & Company
979 3rd Ave. #915
New York, NY 10022
Telephone 212.888.7900
traversinc.com

Zimmer + Rohde
15 Commerce Rd.
Stamford, CT 06902
Telephone 203.327.1400
zimmer-rohde.com
Garden Ornaments

GARDEN ORNAMENTS

Archiped Classis
154 Glass St. #100
Dallas, TX 75207
Telephone 214.748.7437
archipedclassics.com

Barbara Israel Garden Antiques
296 Mount Holly Rd.
Katonah, NY 10536
Telephone 212.744.6281
By Appointment Only
bi-gardenantiques.com

Elizabeth Street Gallery
209 Elizabeth St.
New York, NY 10012
Telephone 212.941.4800
elizabethstreetgallery.com

Lexington Gardens
1011 Lexington Ave.
New York, NY 10021
Telephone 212.861.4390
lexingtongardensnyc.com

Pittet Architecturals
318 Cole St.
Dallas, TX 75207
Telephone214.651.7999
pittetarch.com

Tancredi & Morgen
7174 Carmel Valley Rd.
Carmel Valley, CA 93923
831.625.4477
tancredimorgen.com

Treillage, Ltd.
418 E. 75th St.
New York, NY 10021
Telephone 212.535.2288
treillageonline.com

IRON WORK

Brun Metal Crafts, Inc.
2791 Industrial Ln.
Bloomfield, CO 80020
Telephone 303.466.2513

Cole Smith, FAIA and ASID
Smith, Ekblad & Associates
2719 Laclede St.
Dallas, TX 75204
Telephone 214.871.0305
smithekblad.com

Lush fabrics flow from the brush of Houston-based artist Allan Rodewald, turning the heads of those on their way to l'atelier of Interiors by BLP.

Iron Age Studios
4528 Crosstown Expwy.
Dallas, TX 75223
Telephone 214.827.8860
ironagemetal.com

Ironies
2222 Fifth St.
Berkeley, CA 94710
Telephone 510.644.2100
ironies.com

Murray's Iron Work
1801 E. 50th St.
Los Angeles, CA 90058
Telephone 323.521.1100
murraysiw.com

Potter Art Metal
4827 Memphis St.
Dallas, TX 75207
Telephone 214.821.1419
potterartmetal.com

LINENS

Casa Del Bianco
866 Lexington Ave.
New York, NY 10021
Telephone 212.249.9224
casadelbianco.com

Casa di Lino
4026 Oak Lawn Ave.
Dallas, TX 75219
Telephone 214.252.0404
casadilino.com

D. Porthault, Inc.
18 E. 69th St.
New York, NY 10021
Telephone 212.688.1660
d-porthault.com

E. Braun & Co.
484 Park Ave.
New York, NY 10022
Telephone 212.838.0650
ebraunandco.com

Edith Mezard
Chateau de l'Ange
84220 Lumieres Goult
Telephone 33.4.90.72.36.41

Frette
799 Madison Ave.
New York, NY 10021
Telephone 212.988.5221
frette.com

Indulge Maison Decor
2903 Saint St.
Houston, TX 77027
713.888.0181
indulgedecor.com

Léron Linens
D&D Building
979 Third Ave., Ste. 1521
New York, NY 10022
Telephone 212.753.6700
leron.com

Elevating the ordinary, polished brass grills with scroll motifs adorn heating vents throughout the house.

Matouk
925 Airport Rd.
Fall River, MA 02720
Telephone 508.997.3444
matouk.com

Pratesi
829 Madison Ave.
New York, NY 10021
Telephone 212.288.2315
pratesi.com

Sharyn Blond Linens
2718 W. 53rd St.
Fairway, KS 66205
Telephone 913.362.4420
sharynblondlinens.com

Yves Delorme
1725 Broadway Ave.
Charlottesville, VA 22902
Telephone 800.322.3911
yvesdelorme.com

LIGHTING, LAMPS, AND CUSTOM LAMP SHADES

Ann Morris Antiques
239 E. 60th St.
New York, NY 10022
Telephone 212.755.3308

Bella Shades/Bella Copia
255 Kansas St.
San Francisco, CA 94103
Telephone 415.255.0452

Brown
2940 Ferndale St.
Houston, TX 77098
Telephone 713.522.2151
theshopbybrown.com

Cele Johnson Custom Lamps
1410 Dragon St.
Dallas, TX 75207
Telephone 214.651.1645

Marvin Alexander, Inc.
315 E. 62nd St., 2nd Fl.
New York, NY 10065
Telephone 212.753.1084
marvinalexander.com

Murray's Iron Work
1801 E. 50th St.
Los Angeles, CA 90058
Telephone 323.521.1100
murraysiw.com

Nesle Inc.
38-15 30th St.
Long Island City, NY 11101
Telephone 212.755.0515
nesleinc.com

Niermann Weeks
Fine Arts Building
232 E. 59th St., 1st Fl.
New York, NY 10022
Telephone 212.319.7979
niermannweeks.com

Panache
719 N. La Cienega Blvd.
Los Angeles, CA 90069
Telephone 310.652.5050

Paul Ferrante, Inc.
8464 Melrose Pl.
Los Angeles, CA 90069
Telephone 323.653.4142
paulferrante.com

Pettigrew Associates
1715 Market Center Blvd.
Dallas, TX 75207
Telephone 214-745-1351
pettigrew-usa.com

Thomas Grant Chandeliers, Inc.
1804 Hi Line Dr.
Dallas, TX 75207
Telephone 214.651.1937
thomasgrantchandeliers.com

Vaughan Designs, Inc.
979 Third Ave., Ste. 1511
New York, NY 10022
Telephone 212.319.7070
vaughandesigns.com

STONE AND TILE

Ann Sacks Tile & Stone Inc.
8120 N.E. 33rd Dr.
Portland, OR 97211
Telephone 800.278.8453
annsacks.com

Architectural Design Resources
2808 Richmond Ave., Ste. E
Houston, TX 77098
Telephone 713.877.8366
adrhouston.com

Country Floors
15 E. 16th St.
New York, NY 10003
Telephone 212.627.8300
countryfloors.com

Galerie Origines
15 Rue des Saints-Peres
F 75006 Paris
Telephone 33.144.501.515
galerie@origines.fr

M.A. Tile & Stone Design
2120 Las Palmas Dr., Ste. H
Carlsbad, CA 92011
Telephone 760.268.0811

Paris Ceramics USA Inc.
314 Wilson Ave.
Norwalk, CT 06854
Telephone 203.852.8998
parisceramicsusa.com

Renaissance Tile & Bath
349 Peachtree Hills Ave., N.E.
Atlanta, GA 30305
Telephone 800.275.1822
renaissancetileandbath.com

Roof Tile & Slate Company
1209 Carroll St.
Carrollton, TX 75006
Telephone 972.446.0005
claytile.com

Tesserae Mosaic Studio, Inc.
1111 N. Jupiter Rd., Ste. 108A
Plano, TX 75074
Telephone 972.578.9006
tesseraemosaicstudio.com

Unique Stone Imports
1130 W. Morena Blvd.
San Diego, CA 92110
Telephone 619.275.8300
uniquestoneimports-sd.com

Walker Zanger, Inc.
8901 Bradley Ave.
Sun Valley, CA 91352
Telephone 877.611.0199
walkerzanger.com

Waterworks
60 Backus Ave.
Danbury, CT 06810
Telephone 800.899.6757
waterworks.com

TRIMMINGS AND PASSEMENTERIE

Ellen S. Holt, Inc.
1013 Slocum St.
Dallas, TX 75207
Telephone 214.741.1804
ellensholt.com

Houlès USA Inc.
8584 Melrose Ave.
Los Angeles, CA 90069
Telephone 310.652.6171
houles.com

Janet Yonaty
8642 Melrose Ave.
West Hollywood, CA 90069
Telephone 310.659.5422
janetyonaty.com

Kenneth Meyer Company
325 Vermont St.
San Francisco, CA 94103
Telephone 415.861.0118
kennethmeyer.com

Le Potager
108 W. Brookdale Pl.
Fullerton, CA 92832
Telephone 714.680.8864

Leslie Hannon Custom Trimmings
665 Vetter Ln.
Arroyo Grande, CA 93420
Telephone 805.489.8400
lesliehannontrims.com

M & J Trimmings
1008 6th Ave.
New York, NY 10018
Telephone 212.391.6200
mjtrim.com

Renaissance Ribbons
PO Box 699
Oregon House, CA 95962
Telephone 530.692.0842
renaissanceribbons.com

Samuel & Sons
983 Third Ave.
New York, NY 10022
Telephone 212.704.8000
samuelandsons.com

West Coast Trimming Corp.
7100 Wilson Ave.
Los Angeles, CA 90001
Telephone 323.587.0701

Text © 2010 by Betty Lou Phillips
Photographs © 2010 Dan Piassick except:
Betty Lou Phillips © 2010 pages 4, 10, 189, 220, and 221
Ken Harbert © 2010 page 239

Published by
Gibbs Smith
P.O. Box 667
Layton, Utah 84041
1.800.835.4993 orders
www.gibbs-smith.com

Gibbs Smith books are printed on either recycled,
100% post-consumer waste, FSC-certified papers
or on paper produced from a 100% certified
sustainable forest/controlled wood source.

First Edition
14 13 12 11 10   5 4 3 2

Designed by Cherie Hanson
Printed and bound in China

Library of Congress Cataloging-in-Publication Data

Phillips, Betty Lou.
French impressions / Betty Lou Phillips ;
photography by Dan Piassick. —
1st ed.
p. cm.
ISBN-13: 978-1-4236-0456-3
ISBN-10: 1-4236-0456-3
1. Interior decoration—United States—
History—21st century. 2.
Decoration and ornament—France—
Influence. I. Piassick, Dan. II. Title.
NK2004.15.P555 2010
747—dc22
                                    2010015068

Directory

Driven by a single vision that included an imagined end, a team of professionals created a grand *maison* with the spirit of another time and place. Drawing inspiration from *châteaux* throughout the Loire Valley, and then adding modern conveniences, of course, resulted in a new construction with elegant proportions, rich in architectural details and the underpinnings of age. The house revels in limestone imported from France, a slate roof that is antique, reclaimed wood floors and plaster walls and ceiling, which boast historic finishing techniques. Interiors appear fresh—with a bona fide old-world look, as most all the wood pieces are old—some very old. The landscaping is indeed worthy of the French monarchy.

ARCHITECT
Larry E. Boerder
Larry E. Boerder & Associates
4514 Cole Avenue, Suite 101
Dallas, TX 75205
Telephone: 214.559.2285
www.larryboerder.com

CONTRACTOR
John Sebastian
The Sebastian Construction Group
4808 Cole Avenue, Suite 215
Dallas, TX 75205
Telephone: 214.528.4130
www.sebastiancg.com

John Sebastian
The Sebastian Construction Group
2300 Westwood Boulevard, Suite 100
Los Angeles, CA 90064
Telephone: 310.475.7576
www.sebastiancg.com

INTERIOR DESIGN
Interiors by BLP
Betty Lou Phillips, ASID
Andrea Smith, ASID
4200 St. Johns Drive
Dallas, TX 75205
Telephone: 214.599.0191
www.bettylouphillips.com

LANDSCAPE ARCHITECTS
Harold Leidner Company
1601 Surveyor Boulevard
Carrollton, TX 75006
Telephone: 972.418.5244
www.haroldleider.com